FOUNDATIONS OF LITERARY THEORY

The Eighteenth Century

Printed in Great Britain by
Antony Rowe Ltd, Chippenham, Wiltshire

AN ESSAY ON ORIGINAL GENIUS

[redacted]

William Duff

With a new Introduction by
John Valdimir Price

ROUTLEDGE/THOEMMES PRESS

Published in 1994 by

Routledge/Thoemmes Press
11 New Fetter Lane
London EC4P 4EE

Foundations of [redacted]heory : The Eighteenth Century
6 Volumes[redacted]415 10504 8

Routledge/Thoemmes Press is a joint imprint of Routledge and Thoemmes Antiquarian Books Ltd.

Publisher's Note

These reprints are taken from original copies of each book. In many cases the condition of those originals is not perfect, the paper, often handmade, having suffered over time and the copy from such things as inconsistent printing pressures resulting in faint text, show-through from one side of a leaf to the other, the filling in of some characters, and the break up of type. The publisher has gone to great lengths to ensure the quality of these reprints but points out that certain characteristics of the original copies will, of necessity, be apparent in reprints thereof.

INTRODUCTION

In the eighteenth century, the word 'genius' often had a more classical and pagan connotation than we associate with it in the late twentieth century. A 'genius' was the tutelary god given to each person at his or her birth and who thus shaped that person's circumstances, character, and fortune. Or it could be used in the sense that Alexander Pope used it in his 'Epistle to Burlington', (1731) where the landscape gardener is enjoined to

Consult the Genius of the Place in all;
That tells th' Waters or to rise, or fall. (57–8)

In other words, a location, a person, even a thing has about it some defining, unique quality that will distinguish it in its development and expression from others in a similar category. John Dryden in various critical works invokes the idea of genius to mean an aesthetic or an intellectual skill or ability in a person that goes beyond talent and expertise. In his biography of Jonathan Swift, Sir Walter Scott attributes to Swift an often-quoted remark about *A Tale of a Tub* – 'Good God! what a genius I had when I wrote that book' – that iterates the feelings a creative writer might have about his or her accomplishment. Swift's alleged remark is also a bit ambiguous: he may very well have been thinking of some tutelary agent that enabled him to write that puzzling and exasperatingly witty work; or he could have been alluding to that remarkable creative vitality that we find in his major works. As aesthetics began to develop more and more into a discipline or 'science' of its own, the usefulness and suggestiveness of the concept of genius began to be exploited.

The popularity of the idea in the early eighteenth century can, as with many notions and judgements, be traced back to Joseph Addison in *The Spectator* (1711–14). In *Spectator* 160, he mocked scribblers and witlings who were routinely described as geniuses. For Addison, all geniuses seem to have been found in antiquity and achieved their reputations 'by the meer Strength of natural Parts, and without any Assistance of Art or Learning' and who thus 'produced Works that were the Delight of their own Times and the Wonder of Posterity'.[1] The idea that genius could be a freely occurring, unaided faculty that led its possessor into creative and awe-inspiring achievements would become increasingly important in the eighteenth century; indeed, it became something positively to be searched for, and to be encouraged and preserved when found. This is not to suggest that everyone was unreservedly happy with the idea or that it became inspissated with favourable connotations. Henry Fielding seems to have mistrusted the way the term was being bandied about as much as Addison did, though in a more elaborately ironic way. In the introductory chapter to the fourteenth book of *Tom Jones* (1749), he alludes to those who 'by the wonderful Force of Genius only, without the least Assistance of Learning, perhaps,

[1] *The Spectator*, ed. Donald F. Bond (Oxford: The Clarendon Press, 1965), ii, pp. 126–7.

without being well able to read, have made a considerable Figure in the Republic of Letters '.[2] In artistic terms, genius was something of an *objet trouvé*, a phenomenon which expressed itself without benefit of education, training, refinement, learning, or any other similar qualities; and there were doubtless writers who felt that genius was, as Thomas Edison asserted in his autobiography (1932), ninety-nine per cent perspiration and one per cent inspiration.

Edward Young is often regarded as the eighteenth-century author who did the most to bring the concept of genius into the arena of respectable literary theory, in his *Conjectures on Original Composition* (1759). There he more-or-less conflates the words 'genius' and 'original', though the latter derives from the former. Young limits the true manifestations of originality and genius to very few artefacts or compositions, but his work conspicuously affected aesthetic theorizing in the later eighteenth century and the early nineteenth century, especially in Germany.[3] The soil, however, which Young tilled, if I may use one of his own metaphors, had already been well prepared before he published his thoughts. In 1750, George Allen published a very short (eighteen pages) pamphlet, *Some Occasional Thoughts on Genius*, which was little noticed. More substantial was an equally elusive work by William Sharpe, Vicar of Long Burton, whose 140 pages are happily summed up by its comprehensive title: *A Dissertation upon Genius: Or, an Attempt to shew that the Several Instances of*

[2] Henry Fielding, *The History of Tom Jones*, ed. Martin C. Battestin and Fredson Bowers (Oxford: The Clarendon Press, 1974), ii, p. 739.

[3] See Jonathan Bate, 'Shakespeare and Original Genius', in *Genius: The History of an Idea*, ed. Penelope Murray (Oxford: Basil Blackwell, 1989), p. 88.

Distinction, and Degrees of Superiority in the Human Genius are not, fundamentally, the Result of Nature, but the Effect of Acquisition (1755). Sharpe's book is reasonably well argued, but he was clearly writing against the spirit of the time, which was searching for untutored revelations of ability. This cultural primitivism is, of course, quite well known, and it perhaps reached it most excitable and controversial manifestation in the Ossianic controversy.[4]

William Duff contributed more to the shaping of ideas of genius and their later modifications and transformations in aesthetic theories in the nineteenth century than any other British writer, yet he is a strangely neglected figure in studies in the history of ideas.[5] He was born in Aberdeenshire in 1732 and apparently spent all his life there. Trained as a theologian, he took up his first ecclesiastical post in 1755 and continued to serve the church until his death in 1815. *An Essay on Original Genius* (1767) was his first book, which was followed in 1770 by another developing the ideas expressed there, *Critical Observations on the Writings of the most celebrated Original Geniuses in Poetry*. A second edition of the *Essay* came out in the autumn of 1767, with a new four-page dedication to George, Lord Lyttelton, which is reprinted after this introduction. Except for the pagination, this appears to be the sheets of the first edition, or a re-impression of the first edition, with a

[4] See Howard Gaskill, ed., *Ossian Revisited* (Edinburgh: Edinburgh University Press, 1991), passim.

[5] For example, he is not even mentioned in an otherwise estimable collection of essays, *Aberdeen and the Enlightenment*, ed. Jennifer J. Carter and Joan H. Pittock (Aberdeen: The University Press, 1987).

cancel title-page and the two leaves of Dedication. Although the Dedication is no more fulsome than other dedications in this period, the reviewer (below) who disapproved of Duff's metaphor 'ingredients of genius' might just have admired the adroit consistency, if not the slyness, of the image in its second paragraph ('sheltering', 'screened', 'veil'). Duff published sermons as well as a novel, *The History of Rhedi, the Hermit of Mount Ararat* (1773). Although the two books on genius were influential, perhaps an even more influential work appeared in the early nineteenth century, *Letters on the Intellectual and Moral Character of Women* (1807). At least seven further editions appeared in the nineteenth century.[6] Duff's basic argument in both books on genius, that genius is a rare and precious commodity, likely to be contaminated by education is perfectly straightforward; the feelings that genius engages and the passions that it engenders are too easily softened and dissipated by exposure to learning and inquiry.

Despite the existence of a public ready and eager with enthusiasm for genius both as an aesthetic criterion and a creative phenomenon, the London reviewers were rather sniffy about Duff's performance. *The Critical Review: Or, Annals of Literature* carried a notice of the book in its May issue. It began by taking issue with Duff's language: the first section on the 'ingredients of genius' led the reviewer to wish that 'the author had changed the title

[6] See Christine Battersby, *Gender and Genius: Towards a Feminist Aesthetics* (London: The Woman's Press, 1989), pp. 78–9. See also the reprint of *Letters on the Intellectual and Moral Character of Women*, with an introduction by Gina Luria (New York and London: Garland, 1974).

of the section, which gives us an idea of an apothecary's prescription. We all know that genius contains certain characters, but we entertain some doubts, whether the *ingredients of genius* is a term critically admissible in writing.' This cavil at least has the merit of indicating that the topic was one which the reviewer, along with almost anyone interested in 'polite' literature and learning, regarded as so relevant to aesthetic inquiries of the time as not to need stating. Although Duff was 35 when the work was published, the reviewer is 'inclined to suspect that he is a young [author]', without, however, wishing to belittle his undertaking or to discourage him. Yet his next remark indicates that Duff is thick in the middle of a controversy, or at least, in some confusion about the precise definitions of two of the eighteenth century's most popular and crucial critical terms, taste and judgement: 'the operations he describes in the man of judgement are precisely those which contribute to form the character of a man of taste; while the properties he allows to the latter, without having the least connection with taste, only regard feelings.' Much of the interest in aesthetic theory in the eighteenth century lies in the fecundity of the concepts and terms invented, redefined, or resurrected in a search to give literature, art, and to a lesser extent music, the same truth-value that was to be found in the physical sciences.

The review is, as usual, taken up with a good deal of quotation and very little appraisal or even summary. Nevertheless, it documents just how neatly, if unintentionally, Duff had put his finger on some of the impulses that were to be found in eighteenth-century enthusiasm for difficult philosophical texts: 'Though we cannot approve of all this author's opinions and inferences, yet we must acknowledge, that his performance contains many useful and spirited remarks upon compositions of genius; and that it may be perused with great improvement as well as amusement by those readers who want to acquire a knowledge of what is commonly called polite literature.'[7] Several of the authors from whom Duff takes his examples in this volume are familiar classical figures (Homer, Terence, Virgil), but he is also keen to attribute genius to contemporary authors: there is an agreeable proselytizing element in the work on behalf of recent literature that appears more emphatically in the later *Critical Observations*.

Duff's awareness of the classical origins of the idea of genius and his exemplary knowledge of classical philosophy and philology seems to have had the effect of dulling the critical faculties of the reviewer in *The Monthly Review*. Here the review covers some six pages, but the chief assessment comes in the first three sentences: 'The Author of this essay has, with tolerable order and clearness, collected and arranged the several opinions of Aristotle, Longinus, Cicero and Quintilian on the subject he treats of; and has sometimes, though sparingly, interwoven and combined with his discourse the most approved observations in modern criticism. He writes with ease and perspicuity, but is deficient in originality of sentiment. One may read his book without much dissatisfaction; as, in those countries that are not distinguished by uncommon appearances, or unknown objects, though one meets with not great

[7] *The Critical Review: Or, Annals of Literature* (London: A. Hamilton, 1767), xii, pp. 368–74.

entertainment, one may travel at ease while the way is smooth.'[8] Quite the contrary: one of the pleasures of reading Duff's *Essay* lies in the way that it surprises readers who are expecting critical commonplaces. They can be found, of course, but comments such as those about persons 'destitute of Genius' (pp. 158–60) are packed with juxtapositions and assertions that betray an epistemological awareness of the subtleties and intricacies in aesthetic theories that militates against any suggestion of naiveté in Duff.

Late twentieth century awareness of Duff's own 'genius' can be gauged, first, by the fact that this work has been reprinted at least twice in the past thirty years. In a reprint in 1964, John L. Mahoney claimed that Duff's focus on original genius 'suggests a whole approach to art and criticism, an approach that will receive its most eloquent statement in the romantic criticism of Coleridge and Hazlitt'.[9] I would venture to suggest that Duff's definition of genius can be seen to stand on its own, without needing the crutch of being a precursor of Romantic criticism. However, that attitude is not uncommon. James Engell discusses Duff's work and Alexander Gerard's slightly later *Essay on Genius* (1774) sympathetically and intelligently, but also asserts that Duff's *Essay* 'contains in embryo several points that later typify romantic criticism'.[10] Even the most committed

[8] *The Monthly Review; or Literary Journal* (London: R. Griffiths, 1767), xxxvi, p. 435.

[9] William Duff, *An Essay on Original Genius*. Ed., John L. Mahoney (Gainesville, Florida: Scholars' Facsimiles and Reprints, 1964), p. vii. Another reprint by the Garland Press, without any introduction, appeared in 1970.

[10] James Engell, *The Creative Imagination: Enlightenment to Romanticism* (Cambridge, Massachusetts: Harvard University Press, 1981), p. 85.

eighteenth-century scholar is not going to deny the importance or the influence that Duff (and Gerard) had both for British and continental aestheticians in the nineteenth century; but this habit can all too easily have the effect of 'mining' Duff for the pure gold of Romantic wisdom and ignoring his other outstanding features and ingenious innovations. The extensiveness and pervasiveness of Duff's interest in the concept of genius was unique in the eighteenth century. He represented, analysed, and commented on it in a variety of ways, all of which have something to say about its importance as a critical concept and its evaluative utility. It was an idea that lay behind a number of practical criticisms of literature and the fine arts in the eighteenth century, and Duff spelled out the assumptions and the implications in greater detail than any writer before or after him.

John Valdimir Price
Honorary Fellow,
University of Edinburgh, 1994

To the Right Honourable
George Lord Lyttelton.

My Lord,

I beg leave to dedicate to your Lordship the following ESSAY ON ORIGINAL GENIUS, as a public though inconsiderable Testimony of that great Respect which I bear to your Character as a Man, and to Your Abilities as a Writer; and as a Testimony of the grateful Sense I have of the early Notice Your Lordship was pleased to take of this little Work, by bestowing upon it such Approbation as does me real Honour. Your will excuse, my Lord, the mentioning this Circumstance, not only as it partly suggests the proper Apology for the present Address, for which I have already obtained your Permission, but as it is highly gratifying to the Vanity (shall I call it?) or (if Your Lordship will allow me to give it a softer Name) to a natural Desire which I cannot but feel, and which in this case I cannot think blameable, of having it known that this ESSAY hath been distinguished by the favourable Recommendation of my LORD LYTTELTON.

I consider it, my Lord, as a Circumstance peculiarly fortunate, that by sheltering the following ESSAY under Your Lordship's Patronage, it must of consequence be in a great measure screened from the Assaults of the malevolent Part of Mankind; since I am authorised to acquaint then, that Judgement is already passed on it by a Nobleman, whose verdict they will be compelled to revere. At the same time I am not so blind or partial to the Errors of my Performance, as not to have discovered several Faults, which however neither my Health nor Leisure can well allow me to correct. These, and many others which have escaped my Attention, will probably occur to Your Lordship; but I reflect with Pleasure, that Your Benevolence and Candor are equal to Your Discernment, and that the former Qualities will incline you to throw a veil over the Defects which You cannot but perceive.

I will not offend Your Lordship's Delicacy, by attempting the least Sketch of a character which the Public in general holds in Veneration. One distinguishing Part of it, which the Impulse of Gratitude prompts me to dwell on, You will allow me to mention upon this Occasion. It has always been, I had almost said Your Lordship's singular Honour, to have patronised as well as cultivated the Arts and Sciences with uncommon Assiduity. This Part of Your conduct, my Lord, as it cannot fail to endear Your Name to the literary Part of Mankind in particular, so it will reflect a Lustre upon Your Character, which neither Titles nor Opulence can ever confer; and I make no doubt that You will be ranked by Posterity in the same List with that amiable and accomplished Nobleman, who is said to have been ‘the Patron of Literature, and the Darling of the Muses’,[*] in that turbulent Period in which it was his Misfortune to have lived. That You, my Lord, born in a happier íra, in an Age of civil and religious Liberty, may ever continue to be the Promoter of Learning, as well as of

* Lord FALKLAND.

every elegant and useful Art; and that You may shine an Example of public and private Virtue, amidst the Degeneracy of the Times, is the ardent wish of him, who has the Honour to be, with the highest Respect and Gratitude,

My LORD,
Your Lordship's
Most obedient and
Most faithful Servant,
William Duff.

Oct. 30, 1767

AN ESSAY ON ORIGINAL GENIUS;

AND ITS

VARIOUS MODES OF EXERTION

IN

PHILOSOPHY

AND THE

FINE ARTS,

PARTICULARLY IN

POETRY.

Nullius addictus jurare in verba magistri. HORAT.

LONDON:

Printed for EDWARD and CHARLES DILLY in the *Poultry*, near the *Mansion-House*.

MDCCLXVII.

ADVERTISEMENT.

TO explain the nature of GENIUS, to point out its essential ingredients, to shew the respective and the combined efficacy of those ingredients in composition, as well as in the researches of Science and the inventions or improvements of Art, is the principal design of the following Essay. It is of little importance for the Reader to know what were the Author's motives for its publication, or how it comes to be offered to the Public in its present form. Thus far however it may not be improper to acquaint him, that though the Author had at firſt reſolved to confine his views to the conſideration of the ingredients, exertions, and effects of ORIGINAL POETIC GENIUS alone, he was, upon maturer deliberation, inclined to extend his proſpects; and, by taking a more extenſive ſurvey of his ſubject, was deſirous to render the deſign of the Eſſay more complete. He acknowledges likewiſe, that he was partly led on to this method of proſecuting his plan by gradual and almoſt imperceptible ſteps; finding his ſubject growing upon him while he contemplated it nearly, and new proſpects opening themſelves to the imagination, in proportion to the progreſs he had made. As he had not therefore fixed his attention wholly on any particular ſpecies of Genius, ſo as to exclude altogether the conſideration of any other ſpecies; and as he hath taken occaſion to explain both the general nature and the peculiar modifications of this quality, as exerted in the various provinces of Imagination, with various degrees of energy; he reſolved to intitle his performance AN ESSAY ON ORIGINAL GENIUS; which title he thought would be moſt expreſſive of its deſign, and include under it the ſeveral kinds of Genius treated of in the courſe of the following Diſſertation. At the ſame time it cannot but be obſerved, that the Author hath kept the main object of his attention principally in his eye; that he hath more particularly explained the nature, as well as marked the indications and efforts of ORIGINAL POETIC GENIUS, than thoſe of any other mode of this quality; and that the remarks which he hath made upon its other modes and degrees, are like ſo many lines meeting in one central point, to which the eye is directed as the termination of its proſpect.

IT will likewiſe be obſerved, that in this view the Firſt Book may very properly be conſidered as an Introduction to the Second, in which the ſubject is branched out into its various parts, and more particularly diſcuſſed. In the firſt ſection of the former, the objects and ingredients of Genius are inquired into, as well as the efficacy of thoſe ingredients in compoſition;

composition; and if, in explaining the nature or enumerating the ingredients of Genius, the Author hath dissented either from the general opinion, or from the opinion of a few individuals, who may possibly think Genius properly constituted by Imagination alone, he hath produced the reasons on which his sentiments are founded. In the second section, he hath pointed out the usual indications of the above-mentioned quality, considered in a general view; and, in the third, hath entered into a disquisition on a subject nearly connected with it, that of Wit and Humour. The fourth section is appropriated to an inquiry into the mutual influence of Imagination on Taste, and of Taste on Imagination, considered as ingredients in the compoſition of Genius; and the laſt ſection of the firſt book is employed in inquiring into its different degrees and modes of exertion.

HAVING thus laid the foundation, the Author riſes a ſtep higher, and endeavours to explain the nature of that degree of Genius which is properly denominated ORIGINAL; after which he proceeds to conſider its different exertions in Philoſophy, in Poetry, and in the other fine Arts; more particularly pointing out its indications and its efforts in Poetry. Laſt of all, he endeavours to ſhew, that the early and uncultivated periods of ſociety are peculiarly favourable to the diſplay of original Poetic Genius, and that this quality will

ſeldom

ſeldom appear in a very high degree in cultivated life; of which he hath likewiſe attempted to aſſign the reaſons.

SUCH is the general plan of the Eſſay now ſubmitted, with the utmoſt deference, to the judgment and candor of the Public. The Author might avail himſelf of the ordinary practice of ſoliciting an indulgence to the faults of his performance, and he is ſenſible that in many inſtances he ſtands in need of it; but as he does not think it reaſonable to expect an indulgence to faults, which either a more accurate examination of his Work would have qualified him to correct; or which, if incorrigible, a proper ſenſe of his own abilities would have enabled him to diſcern; he is under a neceſſity of ap-

pealing

pealing to the impartial judgment of his Readers, however disadvantageous that appeal may be to himself; conscious as he is, that the utmost an Author can hope for, is a candid examination of his compositions, and an equitable decision concerning their genuine merit.

He is at the same time well aware, that in an Essay on Original Genius, Originality of Sentiment will naturally, and may, no doubt, justly be expected; and that where this is altogether wanting, no other excellence can supply the defect. This observation, it must be confessed, furnishes a very severe test for determining the merit of the following production; and indeed the Author is not a little apprehensive of the

the iſſue of a ſtrict examination. In the mean time, though he has already precluded himſelf from the uſual pleas to indulgence, he may at leaſt be allowed to ſuggeſt the difficulty of the attempt, as ſome kind of apology for the defects in the execution. The far greater number even of thoſe who pretend to be poſſeſſed of learning and intellectual accompliſhments, being neither capable nor willing to think for themſelves on any ſubject, are contented to adopt the ſentiments of perſons of ſuperior abilities, that are circulated in books or in converſation, and echoed from mouth to mouth. It may likewiſe be remarked, that it is frequently no eaſy matter to diſtinguiſh the ſentiments that are derived from the ſources above-mentioned, from thoſe that

that are properly original, and are the reſult of invention and reflection united together. A caſual coincidence of ſentiment will ſometimes happen, where not the leaſt imitation was intended; and when this is the caſe, the Author, in whoſe compoſitions it is found, may as juſtly aſſert his claim to Originality, as if no ſuch coincidence had ever exiſted.

To theſe conſiderations, which will in ſeveral inſtances at leaſt account for an accidental SIMILARITY, and even SAMENESS of ſentiments with thoſe of others, ſuppoſing them to have happened in ſome parts of the following Eſſay, the Author of it begs leave to ſubjoin a caution to his Readers: It is, that they would not expect to meet

meet with original ſentiments in thoſe parts of this Eſſay, where it is ſcarce poſſible they ſhould be diſcovered. Thus, for inſtance, in enumerating the ingredients, pointing out the objects, or illuſtrating the efforts of Genius, there is very little ſcope afforded for any new track of thought; and thoſe who would form juſt opinions of the above-mentioned articles, muſt think as the beſt Authors who have gone before them have done upon the ſame ſubjects. Other parts of the following Treatiſe certainly afford ſufficient ſcope for original ſentiments; and if the Author has not been ſo happy as to ſtrike out ſome of theſe, he hath indeed laboured in vain, and very much failed in the attainment of his propoſed end.

IF

IF he hath diſcovered a vein of original ſentiment in any part of the following Work, it will probably appear in thoſe ſections wherein he has conſidered the connections betwixt GENIUS, WIT, and HUMOUR; traced the mutual influence of IMAGINATION on TASTE, and of TASTE on IMAGINATION; explained the different modifications, degrees, and exertions of ORIGINAL GENIUS, as appearing in PHILOSOPHY, POETRY, and the other fine Arts; pointed out the PERIOD of SOCIETY moſt favourable to the Diſplay of ORIGINAL POETIC GENIUS in particular, and produced various arguments in ſupport of the poſition he hath advanced. In what degree Originality of Sentiment is really diſcovered on the above-mentioned ſubjects,

jects, muſt be left to the determination of the intelligent and impartial Reader. The Author, for his own part, can at leaſt declare, that he is not conſcious of having borrowed his obſervations on theſe ſubjects from the Writings of any other perſon whatever.

SHOULD the volume now offered to the Public, be ſo happy as to obtain its approbation, another will ſoon ſucceed; in which the principal deſign of the preſent volume will be farther purſued, wherein the obſervations on ORIGINAL POETIC GENIUS contained in it, will be exemplified by quotations from the Works of the greateſt original Geniuſes in Poetry, whether ancient or modern.

On

On the other hand, if the present volume should unhappily fall under the public censure, the Author will not be so unreasonable as to remonstrate or complain; for though the public judgment is not infallible, it will for the most part be found to be more just, as it certainly will be more impartial, than the opinion of any Writer concerning the merit of his own productions. That judgment, therefore, even though it should altogether discourage him from the publication of a second volume, he is determined to respect; for he will not obstinately persist in an ill-fated attempt to write, *adversis numinibus*; nor will he discredit himself by publishing what may be thought unworthy of a perusal.

THE

THE

CONTENTS.

BOOK I.

SECTION II.

SECTION III.

SECTION IV.

SECTION V.

BOOK II.

SECTION I.

SECTION II.

SECTION III.

SECTION IV.

Imagination

SECTION V.

Painters,

AN

AN

ESSAY

ON

GENIUS.

BOOK I.

OF THE

NATURE, PROPERTIES, and INDICATIONS

OF

GENIUS;

AND OF ITS

VARIOUS MODES of EXERTION.

SECTION I.

OF THE OBJECTS AND INGREDIENTS OF GENIUS; AND OF THE EFFICACY of thoſe INGREDIENTS UNITED IN COMPOSITION.

IT muſt have occurred to every one who has ſurveyed, with an ordinary degree of attention, the unequal diſtribution of natural talents among mankind; that as there is a great diverſity of theſe obſervable among them, ſo the ſame talents are poſſeſſed in very different proportions by different perſons. This variety both in the kind and degree of mental accomplifhments, while it indicates that man was formed for fociety, doth likewife clearly point out the refpective ftations in life which every individual is beft calculated to fill and to adorn. Education, as it is well or ill directed, may invigorate or weaken the natural powers of the mind, but it cannot produce or annihilate them.

How much foever thefe powers may be perverted or mifapplied, by the folly and ignorance of men, it cannot be denied, that the variety with which they are beftowed, is both a wife and beneficent contrivance of the Author of nature; fince a diverfity and a fubordination of intellectual accomplifhments are no lefs neceffary to the order and good government of fociety, than a fubordination of rank and fortune. By thefe means the general bufinefs of life is moft fuccefsfully carried on; men become mutually dependent upon, and fubfervient to, the neceffities of each other: fome apply themfelves to agriculture and commerce; while

while others, of a more contemplative diſpoſition, or of a more lively imagination, dedicate their time to philoſophy and the liberal arts.

Of thoſe who have applied themſelves to the cultivation of either, a ſmall number only are qualified to extend their empire, and advance their improvement in any conſiderable degree. To explore unbeaten tracks, and make new diſcoveries in the regions of Science; to invent the deſigns, and perfect the productions of Art, is the province of Genius alone. Theſe ends are the objects to which it conſtantly aſpires; and the attainment of theſe ends can only fall within the compaſs of the few enlightened, penetrating, and capacious minds, that ſeem deſtined by Providence for enlarging the ſphere of human knowledge and human happineſs. The bulk of the literary part of mankind muſt be contented to follow the path marked out by ſuch illuſtrious leaders.

Having ſuggeſted the objects to which Genius naturally aſpires, it will be more eaſy to diſcover the means by which it attains them; or, in other words, the principal ingredients which conſtitute this ſingular accompliſhment. Theſe are IMAGINATION, JUDGMENT, and TASTE. We ſhall conſider therefore the peculiar nature of theſe different qualities, and point out the particular efficacy of each, and the combined effects of all, in accompliſhing the purpoſes of Genius.

That Imagination is the quality of all others moſt eſſentially requiſite to the exiſtence of Genius, will univerſally be acknowledged.

Imagination is that faculty whereby the mind not only reflects on its own operations, but which aſſembles the various ideas conveyed to the underſtanding by the canal of ſenſation, and treaſured up in the repoſitory of the memory, compounding or dis-

joining

joining them at pleaſure; and which, by its plaſtic power of inventing new aſſociations of ideas, and of combining them with infinite variety, is enabled to preſent a creation of its own, and to exhibit ſcenes and objects which never exiſted in nature. So indiſpenſibly neceſſary is this faculty in the compoſition of Genius, that all the diſcoveries in ſcience, and all the inventions and improvements in art, if we except ſuch as have ariſen from mere accident, derive their origin from its vigorous exertion *. At the ſame time it muſt be confeſſed, that all the falſe and fallacious ſyſtems of the former, and all the irregular and illegitimate performances in the latter, which have ever

* It would be talking with great impropriety, to aſcribe either the one or the other to the force of an acute and penetrating Judgment; ſince it is the chief province of this faculty, as will immediately be ſhewn, to employ its diſcerning power in demonſtrating, by juſt reaſoning and induction, the truth and importance of thoſe diſcoveries, and the utility of thoſe inventions; while the inventions and diſcoveries themſelves muſt be effectuated by the power of a plaſtic or warm imagination.

been obtruded upon mankind, may be juſtly imputed to the unbounded extravagance of the ſame faculty: ſuch effects are the natural conſequences of an exuberant imagination, without any proportionable ſhare of the reaſoning talent. It is evidently neceſſary therefore, in order to render the productions of Genius regular and juſt, as well as elegant and ingenious, that the diſcerning and coercive power of judgment ſhould mark and reſtrain the excurſions of a wanton imagination; in other words, that the auſterity of reaſon ſhould blend itſelf with the gaiety of the graces. Here then we have another ingredient of Genius; an ingredient eſſential to its conſtitution, and without which it cannot poſſibly be exhibited to full advantage, even an accurate and penetrating JUDGMENT.

The proper office of JUDGMENT in compoſition, is to compare the ideas which imagination collects; to obſerve their agreement or diſagreement, their relations and reſemblances;

blances; to point out ſuch as are of a homogeneous nature; to mark and reject ſuch as are diſcordant; and finally, to determine the truth and utility of the inventions or diſcoveries which are produced by the power of imagination †. This faculty is, in all its operations, cool, attentive, and conſiderate. It canvaſſes the deſign, ponders the ſentiments, examines their propriety and connection, and reviews the whole compoſition with ſevere impartiality. Thus it appears to be in every reſpect a proper counterbalance to the RAMBLING and VOLATILE power of IMAGINATION. The one, perpetually attempting to ſoar, is apt to deviate into the mazes of error; while the other arreſts the wanderer in its vagrant courſe, and compels

† QUINTILIAN, who poſſeſſed all the ingredients of Genius in a high and almoſt equal degree, ſeems to conſider Judgment as ſo eſſential a one in its compoſition, that he will not allow the name of *Invention* to any diſcovery of imagination which has not paſſed the teſt of reaſon: *Nec inveniſſe quidem credo eum qui non judicavit.*

it

it to follow the path of nature and of truth.

Indeed the principal uſe and the proper ſphere of judgment, in works of Genius and Art, is to guard an author or an artiſt againſt the faults he may be apt to commit, either in the deſign or execution of his work, rather than to aſſiſt him in the attainment of any uncommon beauty, a taſk which this faculty is by no means qualified to accompliſh. We may alſo obſerve, that it is chiefly employed in pointing out the moſt obvious blemiſhes in any performance, and eſpecially ſuch as are contrary to the rules of art. There are other blemiſhes, perhaps no leſs conſiderable, that utterly eſcape its notice; as there are certain peculiar and delicate beauties of which it can take no cogniſance. Both theſe are the objects of that faculty which we diſtinguiſhed by the name of TASTE, and conſidered as the laſt ingredient in the compoſition of Genius.

We

"We may define TASTE to be that internal ſenſe, which, by its own exquiſitely nice ſenſibility, without the aſſiſtance of the reaſoning faculty, diſtinguiſhes and determines the various qualities of the objects ſubmitted to its cogniſance; pronouncing, by its own arbitrary verdict, that they are grand or mean, beautiful or ugly, decent or ridiculous *." From this definition it appears, that Taſte is deſigned as a ſupplement to the defects of the power of judgment, at leaſt in canvaſſing the merit of the performances of art. Theſe indeed are the ſubjects on which it exerciſes its diſcerning talent with the greateſt propriety, as well as with the greateſt probability of ſucceſs: its dominion, however, is in ſome degree univerſal, both in the Arts and Sciences; though that dominion is much more abſolute, and more legitimate in the former than it is in the latter.

* Omnes enim, tacito quodam ſenſu, ſine ulla arte aut ratione, quæ ſint in artibus ac rationibus recta ac prava dijudicant. CICERO *de Orat.* lib. iii, cap. 50.

latter. The truth is, to bring philoſophical ſubjects to the tribunal of Taſte, or to employ this faculty principally in their examination, is extremely dangerous, and naturally productive of abſurdity and error. The order of things is thereby reverſed; reaſon is dethroned, and ſenſe uſurps the place of judgment. Taſte therefore muſt be contented to act an inferior and ſubordinate part in the reſearches of ſcience: it muſt not pretend to take the lead of reaſon, but humbly follow the path marked out by it. In the deſigns and works of art, the caſe is quite otherwiſe. Inſtead of being directed by judgment, it claims the direction in its turn; its authority is uncontrolable, and there lies no appeal from its deciſions. Indeed it is well qualified to decide with preciſion and certainty on ſubjects of this kind; for it poſſeſſes a perſpicacity of diſcernment with regard to them, which reaſon can by no means pretend to, even on thoſe ſubjects that are the moſt adapted to its nature. So much more perfect are the ſenſes than the underſtanding.

ſtanding. We ſhall illuſtrate theſe remarks by an example.

Let us ſuppoſe two perſons, the one poſſeſſed of a comprehenſive and penetrating judgment, without any refinement or delicacy of taſte; the other endued with the moſt exquiſite ſenſibility of taſte, without any extraordinary proportion of the reaſoning talent, both ſet to work in examining the merit of ſome maſterly production of art, that admired piece of hiſtory-painting, for inſtance, of the Crucifixion, by MICHAEL ANGELO, and obſerve their different procedure, and the very different remarks they will make. The former meaſures with his eye the exact proportion of every figure in the piece; he conſiders how far the rules of art are obſerved in the deſign and ordonnance; whether the group of ſubordinate figures naturally lead the eye to the capital one, and fix the attention principally upon it; and whether the artiſt has given a proper variety of expreſſion to the countenances of of the ſeveral ſpectators. Upon diſcovering that the painter had exactly conformed to the rules of his art in all theſe particulars, he would not only applaud his judgment, but would alſo give teſtimony to his maſtery and ſkill; without, however, having any true feeling of thoſe uncommon beauties which conſtitute real merit in the art of painting. Such would be the procedure and remarks of the man of mere judgment. Conſider now, on the other hand, in what a different manner the man of taſte will proceed, and in what manner he will be affected. Inſtead of attending, in the firſt place, to the juſt proportions of the various figures exhibited in the draught, however neceſſary to be obſerved; inſtead of remarking, with approbation, the judgment and ingenuity diſplayed by the artiſt in the uniformity of deſign, and in the regularity and juſtneſs that appear in the diſpoſition of the ſeveral figures of the piece; he fixes his eye upon the principal one, in which he obſerves the various contorſions of the countenance, the

natural

natural expreſſions of agoniſing pain, mixed however with an air of divine benignity and compaſſion. Then he paſſes on to the contemplation of the inferior and ſubordinate figures, in which he perceives a variety of oppoſite paſſions, of rage and terror, of admiration and pity, ſtrongly marked in their different countenances; and feels the correſponding emotions in their utmoſt ſtrength which thoſe ſeveral paſſions are calculated to inſpire. In a word, the man of judgment approves of and admires what is merely mechanical in the piece; the man of taſte is ſtruck with what could only be effected by the power of Genius. Whereever nature is juſtly repreſented, wherever the features of any one paſſion are forcibly expreſſed, to thoſe features his attention is attracted, and he dwells on the contemplation of them with intenſe and exquiſite pleaſure. The ſenſations of the former are cool, weak, and unaffecting throughout; thoſe of the latter are warm, vivid, and deeply intereſting; or, to ſpeak more properly,

perly, the one reaſons, the other feels †. But as no reaſoning can enable a man to form an idea of what is really an object of ſenſation, the moſt penetrating judgment can never ſupply the want of an exquiſite ſenſibility of taſte. In order therefore to reliſh and to judge of the productions of Genius and of Art, there muſt be an internal perceptive power, exquiſitely ſenſible to all the impreſſions which ſuch productions are capable of making on a ſuſceptible mind.

This internal power of perception, which we diſtinguiſh by the name of TASTE, and which we have ſhewn to be ſo neceſſary for enabling us to judge properly concerning works of imagination, does not appear to be requiſite, in the ſame degree, in the reſearches of Science. In this department, reaſon reaſſumes the reins, points out and preſcribes

† Non ratione aliqua, ſed motu neſcio an inenarrabili judicatur. Neque hoc ab ullo ſatis explicari puto, licet multi tentaverint. QUINT. *Inſtit.* lib. vi.

the flight of fancy, aſſigns the office, and determines the authority of taſte, which, as we have already obſerved, muſt here be contented to act a ſecondary part. In philoſophical ſpeculations a conſtant appeal is made to the faculty of Reaſon, not to that of Imagination; principles are laid down, arguments are adduced, phenomena are explained, and their conſequences inveſtigated. Hence it follows, that in the whole proceſs judgment is much more exerciſed than taſte. Yet ſome ſcope is alſo afforded for the exerciſe of the latter faculty; for as all diſcoveries in ſcience are the work of imagination, which will be afterwards particularly ſhewn; ſo taſte may be very properly exerted in the illuſtration of thoſe diſcoveries which have obtained the ſanction of reaſon; provided that, in this caſe, taſte and imagination act under the direction, and ſubmit to the controling power of judgment.

On the other hand, judgment has a particular province aſſigned to it, in examining the works of Genius and Art; though, with regard to these, it acts an inferior part, as taste does in the former case. Judgment must not presume to take cognisance of those exquisite and delicate beauties, which are properly the objects of the last mentioned faculty; but it may determine concerning regularity, justness, and uniformity of design, and concerning propriety of sentiment and expression. All these fall within its sphere; and its decisions in these respects command our assent.

Upon the whole; as JUDGMENT and TASTE may be alternately exercised in the sphere of each other, and ought to act with combined influence, though with different power, and with different degrees of exertion; so both these faculties must be united with a high degree of imagination, in order to constitute improved and consummate Genius.

From the observations that have been made on those distinguishing faculties of the human mind,

mind, IMAGINATION, JUDGMENT, and TASTE, it is evident, that not any one of theſe talents, in whatever degree we may ſuppoſe it to exiſt, can of itſelf attain the objects of Genius. Even imagination, the moſt eſſential and predominant ingredient in the compoſition of this character, if we ſuppoſe it to exiſt in a man without any conſiderable proportion of the other faculties, will be miſerably inadequate to the objects juſt mentioned; for though it may, by its own native vigour, ſometimes ſtrike out an important diſcovery, either in ſcience or in art, yet this will no way avail, if there is not a ſufficient ſtrength of reaſon beſtowed to prove its truth and utility. Such a diſcovery will often, however undeſervedly, expoſe the author to ridicule; and the utmoſt reward he can hope for of his labour, is to gain the character of a romantic viſionary, or an adventurous, but vain, projector; though the ſame diſcovery more clearly revealed, and more fully demonſtrated, by another perſon, poſſeſſed perhaps of no higher degree of imagination, but endued with a more penetrating judgment, will procure him that reputation and honour, of which the greateſt part was due to the firſt author.

Having conſidered the nature of the different faculties of IMAGINATION, JUDGMENT and TASTE, and pointed out their reſpective exertions; having alſo ſhewn that imagination, the moſt diſtinguiſhing of theſe faculties, is of itſelf inſufficient to attain the objects of Genius; we ſhall now take a view of Imagination, Judgment, and Taſte, as forming by their union the full perfection of Genius, and ſhall obſerve their combined effects in compoſition.

If we ſuppoſe a PLASTIC and COMPREHENSIVE IMAGINATION, an ACUTE INTELLECT, and an exquiſite SENSIBILITY and REFINEMENT of TASTE, to be all combined in one perſon, and employed in the arts or ſciences, we may eaſily conceive, that the effect of ſuch an union

union will be very extraordinary. In ſuch a caſe, theſe faculties going hand in hand together, mutually enlighten and aſſiſt each other. Imagination takes a long and adventurous, but ſecure flight, under the guiding rein of judgment; which, though naturally cool and deliberate, catches ſomewhat of the ardor of the former in its rapid courſe. To drop the alluſion, imagination imparts vivacity to judgment, and receives from it ſolidity and juſtneſs: TASTE beſtows ELEGANCE on both, and derives from them PRECISION and SENSIBILITY. The effect of the union of theſe qualities in compoſition, will be obſerved and felt by every reader. It will appear in new and ſurpriſing ſentiments, in ſplendid imagery, in juſt and nervous reaſoning, and in eloquent, graceful, and animated expreſſion. Hence, in the writings of an author who poſſeſſes the qualities above mentioned in a high degree, we are convinced, pleaſed, or affected, according to the various ſtrain of his compoſition, as it is adapted to the underſtanding, the imagination, or the heart.

We ſhall not pretend to aſcertain the exact proportion of the ſeveral ingredients which enter into the formation of Genius; it is ſufficient to have ſhewn, that they muſt all ſubſiſt in a conſiderable degree, a truth which we have deduced from the objects of Genius themſelves. We ſhall only remark, that as among the faculties of which Genius is compoſed, imagination bears the principal and moſt diſtinguiſhing part, ſo of courſe it will and ought to be the predominant one. An exact equilibrium of the reaſoning and inventive powers of the mind, is perhaps utterly incompatible with their very different natures; but though a perfect equipoiſe cannot ſubſiſt, yet they may be diſtributed in ſuch a proportion, as to preſerve nearly an equality of weight; and, notwithſtanding the opinion which is generally and abſurdly entertained to the contrary, the powers of imagination and reaſon may be united in a very high degree, though this is not always the caſe, in the ſame perſon.

Should any one be inclined to controvert the account we have given of the nature and ingredients of Genius, and, inſtead of allowing it to be a compound quality, be of opinion that it is conſtituted and characteriſed by Imagination alone; or, in other words, that Genius and Imagination are one and the ſame thing; we ſhall not diſpute with him about words; for the ingredients of Genius depend intirely upon the acceptation in which we take it, and upon the extent and offices we aſſign to it. It is evident, from the idea we have given of its objects, that the ingredients above enumerated and explained, are neceſſary to the attainment of them; and therefore we admit thoſe ingredients into its compoſition. If, after all, any perſon ſhould ſtill continue to think that Genius and Imagination are ſynonymous terms, and that the powers of the former are moſt properly expreſſed by thoſe of the latter; let him reflect, that if the former is characteriſed by fancy alone, without any proportion of judgment, there is ſcarce any means left us of diſtinguiſhing betwixt the flights of Genius and the reveries of a Lunatic.

It is likewiſe to be obſerved, that we regard the *Iliad* and the *Odyſſey* as works of Genius, not only becauſe there appears an aſtoniſhing diſplay of Imagination in the invention of characters and incidents in thoſe admired productions; but alſo, becauſe that Imagination is regulated by the niceſt judgment; becauſe the characters are juſtly drawn, as well as uniformly ſupported; and the incidents as judiciouſly diſpoſed, as they are happily invented: and, laſtly, becauſe regularity and beauty of deſign, as well as maſtery of execution, are conſpicuous throughout the whole. Take away the excellencies now mentioned, and you deprive thoſe divine poems of half their

merit;

merit: deſtitute of theſe excellencies, they could only be conſidered as the rapſodies of an extravagant and lawleſs fancy, not as the productions of well regulated and conſummate Genius.

From all that has been ſaid, one obvious remark naturally ariſes, that induſtry and application, though they may improve the powers of Genius, can never ſuperſede the neceſſity, or ſupply the want of them. The truth of this obſervation is abundantly confirmed by the different ſtrain and ſucceſs of the writings of different authors; which writings ſerve to ſhew, that as Genius is the vital principle which animates every ſpecies of compoſition, the moſt elaborate performances without it, are no other than a lifeleſs maſs of matter, frigid and unintereſting, equally deſtitute of paſſion, ſentiment and ſpirit. To conclude: A performance void of Genius, is like an opake body viewed in a dark and cloudy day; but a perform-

ance

ance irradiated with the beams of this divine quality, is like an object rendered pellucid and tranſparent by the ſplendor of the ſun.

SECTION II.

OF THE USUAL INDICATIONS OF GENIUS.

HAVING endeavoured, in the preceding ſection, to explain the nature, and determine the ingredients of Genius; and having likewiſe pointed out the effects of thoſe ingredients in compoſition, we ſhall now proceed to conſider the moſt uſual indications of the above mentioned quality.

It may be obſerved in general, that Genius is neither uniform in the manner, nor periodical with regard to the time of its appearance. The manner depends upon the original conſtitution and peculiar modification of the mental powers, together with the correſponding organiſation of the corporeal ones, and upon that mutual influence of both, in conſequence of which the mind receives a particular bias to one certain object, and acquires a talent for one art or ſcience rather than another. The period depends ſometimes upon a fortunate accident encouraging its exertion, ſometimes upon a variety of concurring cauſes ſtimulating its ardor, and ſometimes upon that natural efferveſcence of mind (if we may thus expreſs it) by which it burſts forth with irreſiſtible energy, at different ages, in different perſons, not only without any foreign aid, but in oppoſition to every obſtacle that ariſes in its way.

With regard to the firſt of theſe points: though Genius diſcovers itſelf in a vaſt variety of forms, we have already obſerved, that thoſe forms are diſtinguiſhed and characteriſed by one quality common to them all, poſſeſſed indeed in very different degrees,

and

and exerted in very different capacities; this quality, it will be underſtood, is Imagination. The mental powers unfold themſelves in exact proportion to our neceſſities and occaſions for exerciſing them. Imagination therefore being that faculty which lays the foundation of all our knowledge, by collecting and treaſuring up in the repoſitory of the memory thoſe materials on which Judgment is afterwards to work, and being peculiarly adapted to the gay, delightful, vacant ſeaſon of childhood and youth, appears in thoſe early periods in all its puerile brilliance and ſimplicity, long before the reaſoning faculty diſcovers itſelf in any conſiderable degree. Imagination however, in general, exerciſes itſelf for ſome time indiſcriminately on the various objects preſented to it by the ſenſes, without taking any particular or determinate direction; and ſometimes the peculiar bent and conformation of Genius is diſcernible only in the advanced period of youth. The mind, as ſoon as it becomes capable of attending to the repreſentation it receives of outward objects by the miniſtry of the ſenſes, views ſuch a repreſentation with the curioſity of a ſtranger, who is preſented with the proſpect of an agreeable and uncommon ſcene. The novelty of the objects at firſt only affects it with pleaſure and ſurpriſe. It afterwards ſurveys, revolves, and reviews them ſucceſſively one after another; and, at laſt, after having been long converſant with them, ſelects one diſtinguiſhed and favourite object from the reſt, which it purſues with its whole bent and vigour. There are ſome perſons, it is true, in whom a certain bias or talent for one particular art or ſcience, rather than another, appears in very early life; and in ſo great a degree as would incline us to imagine, that ſuch a diſpoſition and talent muſt have been congenial and innate. While perſons are yet children, we diſcover in their infantile purſuits the opening buds of Genius; we diſcern the rudiments of the Philoſopher, the Poet, the Painter, and the Architect.

The

The productions indeed of youthful geniuses will be naturally marked with those improprieties and defects, both in design, sentiment and expression, which result from the florid, exuberant, and undisciplined imagination, that is peculiar to an age wherein Judgment hath not yet exerted its chastening power. When the case is otherwise, and this faculty hath attained considerable maturity in early youth, it affords no favourable presage of future grandeur and extent of Genius; for we rarely find fruit on the tree which puts forth its leaves and blossoms on the first return of spring *. Nature

* QUINTILIAN considers these forward geniuses as hasty and untimely growths, like those ears of corn, which suddenly spring up in a shallow soil, without striking their roots deep into the earth, and acquire the colour, but not the substance of full and ripe grain, before the natural time.

Illud ingeniorum velut præcox genus, non temere unquam pervenit ad frugem. Hi sunt qui parva facile faciunt; & audacia provecti, quicquid illic possunt, statim ostendunt. Possunt autem id demum quod in proximo est:

Nature requires time to mature her productions; the powers of the mind and body grow up together, and both acquire their proper consistence and vigour by just degrees; this at least is the ordinary course of nature, from which there are few exceptions.

But though Genius cannot be said to attain its full perfection till the reasoning faculty, one of its essential ingredients, acquires its utmost extent and improvement; yet there are certain indications of its existence and powers, even in early life, which an attentive observer may easily discover, and which are as various as the forms wherein it appears.

---

est: verba continuant; hæc vultu interrito, nulla tardati verecundia proferunt: non multum præstant, sed cito; non subest vera vis, nec penitus immissis radicibus nititur: ut quæ summo solo sparsa sunt semina, celerius se effundunt & imitatæ spicas herbulæ inanibus aristis ante messem flavescunt. QUINT. *Instit.* lib. i. cap. 3.

We ſhall conſider the moſt diſtinguiſhing of theſe forms, and the peculiar indications which characteriſe them. Let us firſt obſerve the eſſential indications of philoſophic Genius.

Imagination receives a very different modification or form in the mind of a Philoſopher, from what it takes in that of a Poet. In the one it extends to all the poſſible relations of things; in the other it admits only thoſe that are probable, in order to determine ſuch as are real. Hence it ſhould ſeem, that in the firſt inſtance it ought to poſſeſs greater compaſs, and in the laſt, greater accuracy. Here then we have one characteriſtical indication of a Genius for philoſophical Science; and that is, accuracy of imagination. Its aſſociations of ideas will be perfectly juſt and exact, no extraneous ones will be admitted; it will aſſemble all that are neceſſary to a diſtinct conception and illuſtration of the ſubject it contemplates, and diſcard ſuch as are no way conducive to thoſe purpoſes. This preciſion and accuracy in ſelecting and combining its ideas, appears to proceed from a native regularity, clearneſs, and even ſtrength of Imagination, united with a certain *acumen ingenii*, a ſharpneſs of diſcernment, the true criterions of philoſophic Genius.

We may farther obſerve, that though Reaſon, by ſlow and gradual ſteps attains its utmoſt extent of comprehenſion, yet being a very diſtinguiſhing faculty in the mind of the Philoſopher, it appears to advance faſter to maturity in him than in any other perſon; and ſome preſages of the future extent of his underſtanding may be derived from his firſt argumentative eſſays. He will likewiſe diſcover an acuteneſs of perception, a ſhrewdneſs and ſagacity in his obſervations, remarkable for his years; and will begin early to inſtitute compariſons, to connect his ideas, and to judge of the relations in which he ſtands to the perſons and objects with which he is ſurrounded.

This

This ſeems to be the natural progreſs, and firſt exertion of Reaſon, in uſeful Science.

Let it be remarked in the laſt place, that philoſophical Genius is peculiarly diſtinguiſhed by a certain moral and contemplative turn of mind. It feels a powerful tendency to ſpeculation, and derives its chief pleaſure from it. Not ſatisfied with exploring the phenomena of nature, it delights to inveſtigate their unknown cauſes. Such are the uſual indications of philoſophic Genius. We ſhall next conſider the moſt remarkable indications of this character in Poetry.

As Imagination is the predominant ingredient in the compoſition of poetic Genius, it will there diſcover itſelf in its utmoſt exuberance and fecundity. This faculty will naturally diſplay its creative power on thoſe ſubjects which afford fulleſt ſcope for its exerciſe; for which reaſon it will run into the more pleaſing ſpecies of fiction, and will be particularly diſtinguiſhed by a happy fertility of invention. But though fable be the ſtrain of compoſition of all others moſt ſuitable and appropriated to the higheſt claſs of poetic Genius, neither its choice nor its abilities are reſtricted to this alone. It freely indulges itſelf on a variety of ſubjects; in the ſelection of which a Poet is in a great meaſure influenced by his age, temper, and ruling paſſion. Thus poems deſcribing the beauties of nature, the tender tranſports of love, the flattering proſpects of ambition, the affectionate and ardent reciprocations of friendſhip, and the peaceful pleaſures of rural tranquillity, are often among the firſt eſſays of a young Bard. We purpoſely avoid being ſo particular on this branch of our ſubject, as we would otherwiſe chooſe to be, leſt we ſhould anticipate ſome of the obſervations that will be made on the diſtinguiſhing characters of original poetic Genius, in another part of our Eſſay.

It may not however be improper farther to obſerve in this place, that one who is born with a Genius for Poetry, will diſcover a peculiar reliſh and love for it in his earlieſt years; and that he will be naturally led to imitate the productions he admires. Imagination, which in every man diſplays itſelf before any of the other faculties, will be diſcernible in him in a ſtate of childhood, and will ſtrongly prompt him to Poetry: TASSO, we are told, compoſed poems when he was only five years of age; POPE, we know, wrote ſome accurate little pieces, when he was ſcarce twelve; and he himſelf acquaints us, by a beautiful, but doubtleſs figurative expreſſion, that he began to write almoſt as ſoon as he began to ſpeak:

As yet a child, nor yet a fool to fame,
I liſp'd in numbers, for the numbers came.

MILTON dedicated his Genius to the Muſes in his earlieſt youth: he has preſented us with a few poems written in his thirteenth or fourteenth year, inaccurate indeed, as was natural at ſuch an age, eſpecially in one who was afterwards to become ſo great a Poet, but full of the ardor and inſpiration of genuine Poetry. Indeed moſt of his juvenile pieces, which are very unequal in their merit, afford the happieſt preſages of that amazing grandeur and extent of Imagination, of which he long after exhibited ſo glorious a monument in his *Paradiſe Loſt.*

We ſhall only add, that the performances of a youthful Poet, poſſeſſed of true Genius, will always abound with that luxuriance of imagination, and with that vivacity and ſpirit which are ſuitable to his years; but at the ſame time they will generally be deſtitute of that chaſtity and maſculine vigour of expreſſion, as well as juſtneſs and propriety of ſentiment, which are only compatible with maturer age †.

The

† That great Maſter of Reaſon and Eloquence, whom we laſt quoted, and whom we ſhall have frequent

The ſame VIVACITY and ARDOR of Imagination which indicates the Poet, characteriſes

quent occaſion to quote in the courſe of this Eſſay, ſince his ſentiments on the ſubjects of which he treats, are as juſt as they are elegantly and happily expreſſed, obſerves, that luxuriance of Imagination is to be regarded as a favourable indication of future fertility and copiouſneſs of Genius; adviſes that it ſhould by all means be encouraged; and ſuggeſts the proper method of encouraging it, without apprehending any danger from its exceſs.

Nec unquam me in his diſcentis annis offendat ſi quid ſuperfuerit. Quin ipſis doctoribus hoc eſſe curæ velim, ut teneras adhuc mentes more nutricum mollius alant, & ſatiari velut quodam jucundioris diſciplinæ lacte patiantur. Erit illud plenius interim corpus, quod mox adulta ætas aſtringat. Hinc ſpes roboris. Maciem namque & infirmitatem in poſterum minari ſolet protinus omnibus membris expreſſus infans. Audeat hæc ætas plura, & inveniat, & inventis gaudeat, ſint licet illa non ſatis interim ſicca & ſevera. Facile eſt remedium ubertatis, ſterilia nullo labore vincuntur. Illa mihi in pueris natura minimum ſpei dabit, in qua ingenium judicio præſumitur. Materiam eſſe primam volo vel abundantiorem, atque ultra quam oporteat fuſam. Multum inde decoquent anni, multum ratio limabit, aliquid velut uſu ipſo deteretur, ſit modo unde

terises likewise and distinguishes the Painter; the signs only being different by which it is expressed. The former endeavours to impart his sentiments and ideas to us by verbal description; the latter sets before our eyes a striking resemblance of the objects of which he intends to convey an idea, by the ingenious contrivance of various colours delicately blended, and by the proper union of light and shade. In order to effect his purpose, he must have his imagination possessed with very vivid conceptions of the objects he

---

excidi possit & quod exculpi. Erit autem, si non ab initio tenuem nimium laminam duxerimus, & quam cælatura altior rumpat. QUINTIL. *Instit.* lib. ii. cap. 4.

CICERO's sentiments on this subject coincide exactly with those of QUINTILIAN quoted above:

Volo enim, se efferat in adolescente fœcunditas: nam facilius, sicut in vitibus revocantur ea, quæ sese nimium profuderunt, quam, si nihil valet materies, nova sarmenta cultura excitantur: ita volo esse in adolescente unde aliquid amputem. Non enim potest in eo esse succus diuturnus, quod nimis celeriter est maturitatem assecutum. *De Orat.* lib. ii. cap. 21.

would

would thus exhibit; otherwise it is impossible he should delineate the transcript of them upon canvas. The Imagination must guide the hand in the design and execution of the whole. A Painter therefore of true Genius, having his fancy strongly impressed and wholly occupied by the most lively conceptions of the objects of which he intends to express the resemblance, has immediate recourse to his pencil, and attempts, by the dexterous use of colours, to sketch out those perfect and living figures which exist in his own mind. He will be frequently observed to employ his talents in this manner; and the eminence and extent of his Genius is indicated by the degree of his success.

Imagination, in a considerable degree, is also requisite to the Musician, who would become excellent in his profession. He must be thoroughly acquainted with the power of sounds in all their variety of combination. His imagination must assist him in combining ſounds, in order to conſtitute different ſpecies of harmony; and his experience of the effects of various modulations, firſt on the ear, and, by the inſtrumentality of this organ on the paſſions, muſt aid his fancy in ſetting his compoſitions to the notes of muſic. By ſuch exerciſes a muſical Genius is indicated.

A Talent or Genius for Architecture is diſcovered by a proper union of Imagination and Taſte, directed to the accompliſhment of the ends of this art. The degree of Imagination neceſſary to a maſtery in Architecture, depends upon the bounds we aſſign to it, and the improvements we ſuppoſe practicable in it. Human ingenuity hath as yet diſcovered only five orders in this art, which contain all the various forms of grandeur and beauty, conſiſtent with regularity, that have ever been invented; and our modern artiſts have confined their ambition to the ſtudy and imitation of thoſe illuſtrious monuments of

Genius

Genius left them by their predeceſſors, as if it were impoſſible to invent any other ſuperior or equal models. To invent new models of Architecture, would, we confeſs, require great compaſs of Imagination. In ſuch inventions however true Genius delights, and by ſuch it is indicated in a very high degree. To unite in one conſummate plan the various orders of ancient Architecture, requires indeed a conſiderable ſhare of Imagination; but it may be obſerved, that a refined and well formed Taſte is the principal requiſite in a modern Architect; for though Fancy may be employed in combining the different orders of Architecture in one general deſign, it is the province of Taſte alone to review the parts thus combined, and to determine the beauty and gracefulneſs of the whole. Setting aſide, therefore, new inventions in this art, which can only be effected by an uncommon extent of Imagination, we may venture to affirm, that the employment of Fancy and

and Taſte, in the manner above mentioned, is a proper indication of a Genius for Architecture, as well as neceſſary to the accompliſhment of ſuch a Genius.

With reſpect to a Genius for Eloquence, its characteriſtical indications are eſſentially the ſame with thoſe which denote a talent for Poetry *. The ſame creative power, the ſame extent and force, the ſame impetuoſity, and fire of Imagination, diſtinguiſh both almoſt in an equal degree; with this difference only, that the latter is permitted to range with a LOOSER rein than is indulged to the former, which,

* Eſt enim finitimus Oratori Poeta, numeris adſtrictior paulo, verborum autem licentia liberior, multis vero ornandi generibus ſocius ac pene par; in hoc quidem certe prope idem, nullis ut terminis circumſcribat, aut definiat jus ſuum, quo minus ei liceat eadem illa facultate, & copia, vagari qua velit. CICERO *de Orat.* lib. i. cap. 16.

though

though it may dare to emulate the boldneſs and ſublimity of poetic inſpiration, is not allowed to SPORT and WANTON with ſuch WILDNESS and LUXURIANCE.

SECTION III.

OF THE CONNECTION BETWIXT GENIUS, WIT, AND HUMOUR.

GENIUS, WIT, and HUMOUR, have been conſidered by many as words of equivalent ſignification; and have therefore been often injudiciouſly confounded together. Some do not perceive the difference betwixt them; and others, not attending to it, uſe theſe expreſſions alternately and indiſcriminately. There is however a real difference between theſe accompliſhments; and

and as the ſubject of this Section is neither incurious nor unimportant, and is, to us at leaſt, new, we ſhall endeavour in the progreſs of it to explain the nature, and to mark the eſſential and peculiar characters of the above-mentioned qualities: we ſhall point out their diſtinguiſhing difference, and ſhew their mutual connection.

The talents we are treating of are all the offspring of Imagination, of which quality however they participate in very different degrees; as a much greater ſhare of it is requiſite to conſtitute true Genius, than is neceſſary to conſtitute either of the other endowments. Our preſent inquiry obliges us to anticipate a little what will afterwards be more fully diſcuſſed, by remarking, that Genius is characteriſed by a copious and plaſtic, as well as a vivid and extenſive Imagination; by which means it is equally qualified to invent and create, or to conceive and deſcribe in the moſt lively manner the objects it contemplates.

Such

Such is the nature, and ſuch are the eſſential characters of Genius. On the other hand, Wit and Humour neither invent nor create; they neither poſſeſs the vigour, the compaſs, nor the plaſtic power of the other quality. Their proper province is to aſſemble with alertneſs thoſe ſentiments and images, which may excite pleaſantry or ridicule. Hence vivacity and quickneſs of Imagination form their peculiar characters. In fact, the accompliſhments of Wit and Humour, which are ſo much the objects of applauſe and envy, are derived from this vivacity of Fancy, united with an exquiſite ſenſe of Ridicule. As a proof of this, we need only to obſerve, that they are generally employed in painting the ridiculous in characters and in manners; and thoſe flaſhes of wit, and ſtrokes of humour, we ſo much admire, are by no means the effects of a creative Imagination, the diſtinguiſhing characteriſtic of true Genius; but of a quickneſs and readineſs of fancy in aſſembling ſuch ideas as lie latent in the mind, till the combining

combining power of aſſociation, with the aſſiſtance of the retentive faculty, calls them forth, by the ſuggeſtion of ſome diſtant, perhaps but correſponding circumſtance. This ſeems to be no improbable theory of Wit and Humour; which, though akin to each other, and produced by the ſame cauſes, are however diſtinct qualities, and may exiſt ſeparately.

The former is the moſt ſhining, the latter the moſt pleaſing and the moſt uſeful quality. Wit diſcovers itſelf in ſmart repartees, in ingenious conceits, in fanciful alluſions, and in brilliant ſentiments. Humour, on the other hand, manifeſts itſelf in ludicrous repreſentations, in maſterly ſtrokes of manners and character, in ſhrewd obſervations, and in facetious argumentation and narrative. This quality may be divided into two kinds; into that which is diſplayed in the repreſentation of characters, and may be denominated humour of character; and into that which is diſplayed in compoſition, and may be called humour in writing. The first consists in the art of marking the follies, the foibles, or the oddities of the character exhibited so strongly, and exposing them in such a ludicrous light, as to excite pleasantry and laughter. Sometimes the character may be so amiable, that its little peculiarities, instead of lessening our esteem or affection, increase the former, and conciliate the latter; provided however, those peculiarities are innocent in themselves, and indicate or imply genuine excellence. Of this kind is the character of Sir ROGER DE COVERLEY, drawn with the most exquisite humour, and by the happiest effort of ADDISON's delicate pencil.

Humour in WRITING consists either of random strokes of RIDICULE and FACETIOUSNESS, occasionally thrown out, as subjects of DROLLERY and PLEASANTRY happen to occur; or of a vein of IRONY and DELICATE SATIRE, purposely displayed on a particular subject. Perhaps POPE's *Rape of the*

the Lock is the moſt refined piece of HUMOUR in this kind, which any age can boaſt. There remains indeed another ſpecies of Wit and Humour (for it participates of, or at leaſt pretends to both) of the loweſt ſort however, but deſerving ſome attention; that which conſiſts of puns, quibbles, and the petulant ſallies of a rambling and undiſciplined fancy; and which is ſometimes diſplayed in converſation. This ſpecies of it is not only generally oſtentatious, but ſuperficial. It flaſhes for a little while, and then expires. It ruſhes on with precipitation, and, like a ſhallow ſtream, makes a great noiſe; but the rivulet ſoon dries up, and betrays the penuriouſneſs of the ſource from which it flowed. The converſation-wits reſemble thoſe perſons, whoſe ideas paſs through their minds in too quick ſucceſſion to be diſtinct; but who, nevertheleſs, being endued with a natural volubility of expreſſion, acquit themſelves to admiration in company; while one is at a loſs to find either ſenſe or grammar in their compoſitions. To become a man of true Wit and Humour, it is neceſſary to *think*; a piece of drudgery which the Gentlemen we are ſpeaking of are too lively to undergo.

But to return: it appears that WIT and HUMOUR, though nearly ALLIED to true Genius, being the offspring of the ſame parent, are however of a diſtinct nature; ſince the former are produced by the efforts of a RAMBLING and SPORTIVE Fancy, the latter proceeds from the copious effuſions of a plaſtic Imagination. Hence it will follow, that every man of GREAT WIT will not be a GREAT GENIUS, nor will every man of GREAT GENIUS be a GREAT WIT. Theſe qualities do not always exiſt together. Thus SWIFT was not a GENIUS, at leaſt of a very EXALTED kind *, in the ſenſe in which

* Perhaps ſome of the Dean's moſt zealous admirers may be offended with a declaration which excludes his pretenſions to any extraordinary degree of Genius. But

which we have confidered it, nor OSSIAN a Wit. To this perhaps it will be replied, that the Mufe of the latter had caught the complexion of his own temper, which was a melancholy one, partly derived from his natural conftitution, and partly occafioned by the misfortunes of his family; and that his fubjects, being of the mournful kind, could not admit of the fprightly graces of WIT and HUMOUR. But let it be obferved, that

---

But let them reflect on what fuch pretenfions are founded. I can recollect no performance of the Doctor's, which can juftly denominate him a man of great Genius, excepting his *Gulliver* and his *Tale of a Tub*; in which, it muft be confeffed, he hath united both Invention and Humour: and therefore we allow him to have poffeffed a degree of Genius, proportionable to the degree of Invention difcovered in the above mentioned performances. In that kind of wit and humour which he attempted, though not the moft delicate, he unqueftionably excelled all mankind. In the fcale of Genius, however, we muft affign him an inferior ftation; fince his Mufe fcarce ever rifes to the region of the Sublime, which is the proper fphere of a great Genius; but, on the contrary, delights to wallow in the offal and naftinefs of a fty or a kennel.

the melancholy turn of his mind, which irresiftibly determined him to the choice of mournful fubjects, is a fufficient proof that thefe were not only moft fuited to his Genius; but that thofe of a folemn, awful, and pathetic nature, if we include the wild and picturefque, as fubfervient to the others, were the only fubjects in which he was qualified to excel. The lighter ornaments of WIT would have been unfuitable to the fublimity of his Genius, and the penfive turn of his mind. We do not intend to infinuate, that Genius and Wit in the higheft degree are in general incompatible. They were united in SHAKESPEAR almoft in an equal meafure; and YOUNG hath given a fpecimen of the former in his *Night Thoughts*, and of the latter in his *Univerfal Paffion*; and in him they were both united together in a degree of perfection that has not been equalled, fince the era of the great Poet laft mentioned. We only mean to affert, that the one may exift without the other, which we think hath been proved in the cafe of Os-

SIAN

SIAN in particular; though we ſhall readily allow, that the ſimplicity of manners which prevailed in the times of the CALEDONIAN Bard, a ſimplicity that was very unfavourable to the diſplay of WIT and HUMOUR, joined to the melancholy turn of his own temper, heightened by his affliĉtions, might have greatly contributed to ſuppreſs the talents of which we are ſpeaking, ſuppoſing him to have been poſſeſſed of them. We ſhall only add, that there is one caſe in which Wit and Humour may claim the denomination of Genius; and that is, when they are accompanied with a rich fund of invention, as in the *Rape of the Lock*; in which, though the machinery of the Sylphs is not the mere creation of the Poet's fancy, yet the particular nature and employment of thoſe wonderful aerial beings is altogether his own fiĉtion. In this incomparable heroicomical poem, POPE has inconteſtibly eſtabliſhed his charaĉter both as a man of Genius and Wit. It ought however to be remembered, that we allow his title to the first of these denominations, not at all upon account of the vein of delicate and refined satire which runs through the whole poem, for WIT and HUMOUR could have produced this; but upon account of that ingenious INVENTION, and that PICTURESQUE DESCRIPTION, so remarkable in it, which those qualities of themselves could never have produced.

Upon the whole: from the view we have taken of the nature and characters of GENIUS, WIT, and HUMOUR, it appears evident, that as these qualities are in their nature different from each other, and are marked by certain peculiar and distinguishing characters; so they have different spheres of exercise assigned them, in which alone they can display their proper powers to advantage. We may therefore with some appearance of reason infer, that the connection of the above-mentioned talents is only partial and casual, not universal and necessary. This hath in part been already evinced and

and exemplified by particular inſtances; from which it appears, that thoſe talents have been ſometimes united, and ſometimes disjoined in different perſons. As we do not remember to have ſeen this accidental connection, where a neceſſary one at firſt view might be expected, accounted for, we ſhall conclude the preſent Section with endeavouring to aſſign the reaſons of it.

That Genius, Wit, and Humour, do in common participate of Imagination, we have already acknowledged. This participation indeed forms a NATURAL, but not a NECESSARY connection betwixt thoſe qualities. The MODES (if we may ſo expreſs it) and DEGREES of this Imagination are ſo different, and the tempers of men, on which the exertion of the above mentioned qualities greatly depends, are likewiſe ſo various, that a real union becomes merely FORTUITOUS. In order to make this ſtill more evident, as well as farther to account for it, let us recollect the peculiar office of GENIUS,

com-

compared with that of WIT and HUMOUR. The proper office of the former is to INVENT incidents or characters, to CREATE new and uncommon scenery, and to describe every object it contemplates, in the most striking manner, and with the most picturesque circumstances: that of the latter is to represent MEN, MANNERS and THINGS, in such a ludicrous light, as to excite PLEASANTRY, and provoke RISIBILITY. Hence we conclude, that a vigorous, extensive, and PLASTIC Imagination, is the principal qualification of the one, and a quick and lively Fancy the distinguishing characteristic of the other. These qualities do not appear to be connected in any great degree; for what considerable connection is there betwixt a celerity in assembling SIMILAR ideas, together with a lively perception of that SIMILARITY, and the power of inventing a variety of surprising SCENES and INCIDENTS, conceived with the utmost strength and compass of Imagination? It should even seem that on some occasions an extraordinary

nary vivacity of Fancy, which includes a certain degree of volatility, occaſioning the mind to ſtart as it were from one object to another, without allowing it time to conceive any of them diſtinctly, might be prejudicial to that vivid conception, and that extenſive combination of ideas which indicate and characteriſe true Genius. In this caſe, the mind, hurried with precipitancy from one theme to another, though it may catch a glimpſe, yet rarely obtains a full view of the object it deſires to contemplate. This ſeems to be the principal reaſon why GENIUS, whoſe ideas are VIVID and COMPREHENSIVE, is not always united with WIT, whoſe conceptions are QUICK and LIVELY, but frequently SUPERFICIAL.

After all, I am ſenſible that the poſition laid down above, will to many perſons appear extremely problematical; and that ſeveral of thoſe who can perceive the difference betwixt GENIUS and WIT, will ſtill be of opinion, that theſe qualities, however diſtinct

diſtinct from each other, are nevertheleſs indiſſolubly connected. After having reflected a good deal upon the ſubject, the ſentiments I have now delivered are the reſult of that reflection; which ſentiments I have endeavoured to confirm by examples, more of which I could have added, had it appeared to be neceſſary. The truth is, the obſerving that GENIUS and WIT have to all appearance been ſeparately poſſeſſed by different perſons, led me firſt to ſuſpect that their union was caſual. Proceeding upon this principle, I have attempted to aſſign the reaſons of it, which I have deduced from the different natures of thoſe qualities themſelves. Perhaps indeed the examples may appear more convincing than the arguments. I can conceive indeed but one other objection to the former, beſides what has been already ſuggeſted, which is, that men of Genius, conſcious of poſſeſſing ſuperior talents, are not very ambitious of acquiring the reputation which ariſes from WIT. But I cannot think that this anſwer intirely ſolves the difficulty, ſup-

ſuppoſing the union of the above-mentioned qualities really neceſſary; for the reputation acquired by the diſplay of Wit, however inferior this talent may in fact be, is often ſuperior to that which is acquired by the diſplay of Genius; and we may conclude in general, that moſt of thoſe who are poſſeſſed of it, will be deſirous of being diſtinguiſhed upon that account; and conſequently, where it does not diſplay itſelf, that it does not probably in any great degree exiſt. It is neceſſary to remark, in order to prevent any miſtake of my meaning, that while I endeavoured to prove that Genius and Wit are not neceſſarily connected, I had chiefly in my eye that ſpecies of Wit which is the ſudden effuſion of a lively fancy, and which is poured forth in converſation with a ſurpriſing readineſs and exuberance. That real Genius frequently exiſts without this kind of it, I am fully convinced by many examples, which, as the Reader may eaſily recollect them, I ſhall not here enumerate. That kind of Wit and Humour however, which is diſcovered

covered in compoſition, and which being more the effect of thought, is commonly more juſt and ſolid, though often leſs brilliant, Genius will not ſo eaſily reſign its claim to. Indeed, to declare my own opinion upon a doubtful point, where examples contradict each other, it appears to me moſt probable, that true Genius is, we do not ſay, univerſally and neceſſarily, connected with it; but that it rarely exiſts without this kind of Wit; though its exertion may, by various cauſes, in a great meaſure be ſuppreſſed. When theſe qualities are united together, they mutually aſſiſt and improve each other; GENIUS derives VIVACITY from WIT, and WIT derives JUSTNESS and EXTENT of COMPREHENSION from GENIUS.

SECTION IV.

OF THE MUTUAL INFLUENCE OF IMAGINATION ON TASTE, AND OF TASTE ON IMAGINATION; CONSIDERED AS INGREDIENTS in the COMPOSITION OF GENIUS.

WE have already conſidered IMAGINATION and TASTE as two material ingredients in the compoſition of GENIUS. The former we have proved to be the moſt eſſential ingredient, without which Genius

Genius cannot exiſt; and that the latter is indiſpenſibly neceſſary to render its productions ELEGANT and CORRECT.

We are now to ſhew the influence of theſe qualities on each other, and how they contribute by their mutual influence to the improvement and conſummation of Genius. Before we proceed to this diſquiſition, it will be proper to recur to the definition of TASTE, given in a preceding ſection, which, for the ſake of preciſion, we ſhall here repeat. "TASTE is that internal ſenſe, which, by its own exquiſitely nice perception, without the aſſiſtance of the reaſoning faculty, diſtinguiſhes and determines the various qualities of the objects ſubmitted to its cogniſance, pronouncing them, by its own arbitrary verdict, to be grand or mean, beautiful or ugly, decent or ridiculous." The ſimple principles of Taſte are found in every man, but the degrees in which they exiſt, are as various as can well be imagined: in ſome perſons they are weak and rude; in others,

others, they are vigorous and refined. The external organs of ſenſe, which are the original and fundamental principles of Taſte, are indeed nearly the ſame in every one who poſſeſſes in the moſt ordinary degree the eſſential and conſtituent parts of the human frame; but the ideas which are excited in the minds of ſome perſons by the influence of outward objects on the ſenſes, or by the power of reflection, are very different from thoſe excited in the minds of others. Thus two perſons, the one endued with a juſt and elegant taſte, the other almoſt deſtitute of this quality, contemplating a magnificent and well-proportioned building, that of St *Peter*'s, for inſtance, at *Rome*, will be affected in the moſt different manner and degree imaginable. The latter, looking around him with ignorant and inſipid curioſity, caſts his eye on the altar and decorations of the church, which captivate his attention, and pleaſe his rude fancy, merely by their novelty and ſplendor; while he ſtares at the magnificence of the edifice with a foolifh face of wonder. The former, furveying all the fabric together, is ftruck with admiration of the exact fymmetry, and majeftic grandeur of the whole. Or if we fhould fuppofe both to be prefented, at the fame time, with the profpect of a rich, beautiful, and diverfified landfcape, confifting of woods and vallies, of rocks and mountains, of cafcades and rivers, of groves and gardens, blended together in fweet rural confufion; this inchanting fcene would be contemplated by the one with indifference, or at leaft with very little emotion of pleafure, his thoughts being chiefly employed in computing the produce of fo fertile a fpot; while the view of fuch a group of delightful objects would throw the other into rapture. It is natural to afk, whence arifes this amazing difference in their fenfations? The outward organ, by which thefe fenfations are conveyed, is fuppofed to be equally perfect in both; but the internal feeling is extremely different. This difference

muft

muſt certainly proceed from the transforming power of Imagination, whoſe rays illuminate the objects we contemplate; and which, without the luſtre ſhed on them by this faculty, would appear unornamented and undiſtinguiſhed.

The REFINEMENT and SENSIBILITY of Taſte likewiſe, as well as the pleaſures it is calculated to afford, are all derived from the influence of Imagination over this internal ſenſe. By the magical power of Fancy communicated to it, it is qualified to diſcern the beauties of nature, and the ingenious productions of art, and to feel an exquiſitely pleaſing ſenſation from the ſurvey of them. Imagination dwells upon an agreeable object with delight, arrays it in the moſt beautiful colours, and attributes to it a thouſand charms; every repeated view of it increaſes theſe charms; and the Imagination, enraptured with the contemplation of them, becomes enamoured of its own creation. Taſte, catching the contagion from Fancy, contemplates the favourite object with equal tranſport, by which means it acquires and improves its ſenſibility: it becomes more ſuſceptible of pleaſure, and more exquiſitely acute in its ſenſations. Such is the influence of Imagination on Taſte, and ſuch are the advantages which the latter derives from the former.

As true Taſte is founded on Imagination, to which it owes all its refinement and elegance; ſo a falſe and depraved Taſte is often derived from the ſame cauſe. Fancy, if not regulated by the dictates of impartial Judgment, is apt to miſlead the mind, and to throw glaring colours on objects that poſſeſs no intrinſic excellence. By this means it happens, that though the principles of a juſt Taſte are implanted in the mind of every man of Genius, yet, by a neglect of proper cultivation, or too great an indulgence of the extravagant ramblings of Fancy, thoſe principles

principles are vitiated, and Tafte becomes fometimes INCORRECT, and fometimes INDELICATE †. The only method left in fuch a cafe, is to compare the fenfations of Tafte with the objects that produced them, and to correct the errors of this fenfe by an appeal to the dictates of Reafon, in the points where its authority is legitimate; by which means Tafte may attain JUSTNESS and ACCURACY, as by the former exercife it may acquire SENSIBILITY and REFINEMENT, in thofe minds where its principles are implanted in any confiderable degree.

† Let it not be imputed to faftidious, much lefs to malevolent criticifm, if, in order to exemplify the above remarks, we prefume to obferve, that in a work of real Genius, and in which the moft fublime fpirit of Poetry predominates, we mean the *Night Thoughts* of Dr YOUNG, we meet with feveral inftances of falfe tafte, in his antithefes and conceits, which, in a great meafure, debafe the grandeur of fome very noble fentiments.

Having thus pointed out the influence of Imagination on Taſte, let us now conſider the influence of Taſte on Imagination.

As Taste derives all its sensibility and refinement from the prevalence of Imagination, ſo Imagination owes, in a great meaſure, its justness and accuracy to the correct precision of a well regulated Taste. The excurſions of Fancy, undirected by Judgment or Taſte, are always extravagant; and if we ſhould ſuppoſe a compoſition to be conceived and executed by the firſt mentioned faculty alone, it would be an unintelligible rhapſody, a mere maſs of confuſion, compounded of a number of heterogeneous and diſcordant parts. Though Imagination has by far the greateſt ſhare of merit in the productions of Genius, yet, in one view, it may be conſidered as acting a ſubordinate part, as exerting its energy under the prudent reſtrictions of Judgment, and the chaſtening animadverſions

ſions of Taſte. In fact, the proper office of Fancy is only to collect the materials of compoſition; but, as a heap of ſtones, thrown together without art or deſign, can never make a regular and well proportioned building; ſo the effuſions of Fancy, without the ſuperintending and directing powers above-mentioned, can never produce a maſterly compoſition in Science or in Art. Judgment therefore muſt arrange in their proper order the materials which Imagination has collected; and it is the office of Taſte to beſtow thoſe diſtinguiſhing graces, which may give DIGNITY and ELEGANCE to the ſeveral parts, as well as EXCELLENCE and ACCURACY to the whole. Such is the province of Taſte, and ſuch its INFLUENCE on works of Imagination.

From the ſurvey we have taken of the MUTUAL INFLUENCE of theſe different faculties, it appears, that they are equally indebted to each other; and that if, on the one hand, Imagination beſtows SENSIBILITY and REFINEMENT on Taſte, ſo on the other, Taſte imparts JUSTNESS and PRECISION to Imagination; while Genius is conſummated by the proper union of both theſe faculties with that of Judgment, and derives from their combined efficacy all its energy, accuracy, and elegance.

SECTION

SECTION V.

OF THE DIFFERENT DEGREES OF GENIUS, AND ITS VARIOUS MODES of EXERTION.

GENIUS is a word of extenſive and various ſignification. The ſpheres of its exerciſe, and the degrees of its exertion, are very different.

Some perſons poſſeſs ſuch force and compaſs of Imagination, as to be able by the power of this faculty to conceive and preſent to their own minds, in one diſtinct view, all the numerous and moſt diſtant relations of the objects on which they employ it;

it; by which means they are qualified to make great improvements and diſcoveries in the arts and ſciences. The mind in this caſe has recourſe to and relies on its own fund. Conſcious of its native energy, it delights to expand its faculties by the moſt vigorous exertion, Ranging through the unbounded regions of nature and of art, it explores unbeaten tracks of thought, catches a glimpſe of ſome objects which lie far beyond the ſphere of ordinary obſervation, and obtains a full and diſtinct view of others.

We may farther obſerve, that Genius may, in a very conſiderable though much leſs proportion, be diſplayed in the illuſtration of thoſe truths, or the imitation of thoſe models, which it was incapable originally to diſcover or invent. To comprehend and explain the one, or to expreſs a juſt reſemblance of the other, ſuppoſes and requires no contemptible degree of Genius in the Author or Artiſt who ſucceeds in the attempt.

Thus

Thus we allow MACLAURIN, who has explained the Principles of NEWTON's Philoſophy, and STRANGE, who has copied the Cartoons of RAPHAEL, to have been both of them men of Genius in their reſpective profeſſions, though not men of original Genius; for the former did not poſſeſs that COMPASS OF IMAGINATION, and that DEPTH of DISCERNMENT, which were neceſſary to diſcover the doctrines of the *Newtonian* Syſtem; nor the latter that FERTILITY and FORCE of Imagination, that were requiſite to invent the deſign, and expreſs the dignity, grace and energy, diſplayed in the ORIGINALS of the *Italian* Painter.

A certain degree of Genius is likewiſe manifeſted in the more exquiſite productions of the mechanical arts. To conſtitute an excellent Watchmaker, or even Carpenter, ſome ſhare of this quality is requiſite. In moſt of the Arts indeed, of which we are ſpeaking, Induſtry, it muſt be granted, will in a great meaſure ſupply the place of Genius;

nius; and dexterity of performance may be acquired by habit and ſedulous application: yet in others of a more elegant kind, theſe will by no means altogether ſuperſede its uſe and exerciſe; ſince it can alone beſtow thoſe finiſhing touches that bring credit and reputation to the workman. Every ingenious artiſt, who would execute his piece with uncommon nicety and neatneſs, muſt really work from his imagination. The model of the piece muſt exiſt in his own mind. Therefore the more vivid and perfect his ideas are of this, the more exquiſite and complete will be the copy.

In ſome of the mechanical, and in all the liberal Arts, it is not only neceſſary that artiſts ſhould poſſeſs a certain ſhare of Imagination, in order to attain excellence in their different profeſſions; but that ſhare of which they are poſſeſſed, muſt principally turn upon one particular object. It is this BIAS of the mind to one individual art rather than another, which both indicates and con-

conſtitutes what we commonly call a GENIUS for it. This BIAS appears in ſome perſons very early, and very remarkably; and when it does ſo, it ought doubtleſs to be regarded as the ſovereign decree of Nature, marking out the ſtation and deſtiny of her children.

It cannot be denied, that a great degree of Genius is diſcovered in the invention of mechanical arts, eſpecially if they are by the firſt efforts advanced to any conſiderable perfection; for invention of every kind is a ſignal proof of Genius. The firſt inventer of a Watch, an Orrery, or even a common Mill, however ſimple it may now appear in its machinery and ſtructure, was unqueſtionably a man of an extraordinary mechanical Genius. The improvement of theſe inventions is likewiſe a certain criterion of a Genius for them; the degree of which talent is always juſtly rated in proportion to the improvements made by it, conſidered in connection with the art in which they are made.

We

We ſhall not here inquire into the comparative utility and importance of the ſeveral Arts, whether liberal or mechanical, in order to determine the particular degree of Genius requiſite to an excellence in each of them. Let it ſuffice to obſerve in general, that as in the former Imagination hath a wider range, ſo a greater degree of Genius may be diſplayed in theſe than in the other. Hence we infer their ſuperior dignity, tho' perhaps not their ſuperior utility. In the latter indeed, Imagination is very intenſely exerciſed; but it is more confined in its operation: inſtead of rambling from one theme to another, it dwells on a ſingle object, till it has contemplated it fully and at leiſure; whereas in the others, it forms a leſs particular, but more comprehenſive view of the objects ſubmitted to its cogniſance: it takes them in at one glance, though it does not mark their features ſo minutely. A larger compaſs of Imagination therefore is requiſite to conſtitute excellence in the one, and a greater compreſſion of this faculty (if we may

may use the term) to produce eminence in the other.

Genius likewise, when left to follow its own spontaneous impulse, appears in a great variety of forms as well as of degrees. Its modes of exertion are very different. Sometimes it leads to philosophical speculations, and animates the ardor of the Philosopher in his experiments and researches, in his investigation of causes and effects, of the order of Providence, and the constitution of the human mind; and while it points out the objects to which he should direct his studies, it adapts the mental powers to the pursuit, and qualifies them for the attainment of those objects; by communicating that force of imagination, and that depth of discernment which are necessary to his success: at other times, indulging its own native bent, it strikes out a path for itself through the wild romantic regions of Poetry and Fable; and from the infinite variety of objects presented to it in those fields of fiction, selects

ſelects ſuch as are moſt adapted to its nature and powers. Sometimes Genius, ſtill following its own peculiar bias, ſketches out, with a happy fertility of invention, the deſigns of the Painter, and imparts dignity, elegance and expreſſion to the ſeveral figures of his piece. Sometimes it appears to great advantage in the graceful elocution, the impetuous ardor, and the impaſſioned ſentiments of the Orator. Sometimes it diſplays its power in the combination of muſical ſounds. Sometimes it diſcovers itſelf in uniting, by the power of a lively imagination and exquiſite taſte, the various forms of elegance and magnificence in one conſummate model of Architecture. Or, laſtly, taking an humbler aim, it ſometimes unfolds itſelf, not indeed with ſo much power and extent, but ſtill with very conſiderable energy, in the ingenious inventions and exquiſite improvements of the mechanical Arts. So diverſified are the forms of Genius, and ſo various its modes of exertion.

There

There are many indeed, in whom there are no ſtriking ſignatures of this quality diſcernible in any of its forms, who nevertheleſs poſſeſs a conſiderable ſhare of that faculty by which it is chiefly conſtituted. Theſe perſons, poſſeſſing the fundamental qualification of Genius, may, by the force of application, in ſome meaſure ſupply the want of that appropriated Imagination, which confers a talent for one particular art; but can never reach that degree of excellence in their reſpective profeſſions, which a natural impulſe of Genius to its correſponding object, directed with prudence, and aided by proper culture, is calculated to attain. In others, however, the particular indications and EVOLUTIONS of Genius (to uſe a military phraſe) are very remarkable. By attending carefully to theſe SYMPTOMS (if we may alſo adopt a phyſical term) by marking and encouraging their progreſs, Arts and Sciences may be carried to the higheſt degree of perfection, to which human Genius is capable of advancing them.

AN

ESSAY

ON

GENIUS.

BOOK II.

OF

ORIGINAL

GENIUS,

ITS

INDICATIONS, EXERTION,

AND EFFECTS.

SECTION I.

OF THAT DEGREE OF GENIUS, WHICH IS PROPERLY DENOMINATED ORIGINAL.

WE have in the preceding part of this Eſſay treated of Genius in general, and have pointed out its objects, ingredients and effects, as well as ſuggeſted its various modes of exertion. We ſhall now proceed a ſtep higher, and conſider that degree of Genius, which, upon account of its ſuperior excellence, deſerves the name of ORIGINAL. The obſervations we have hitherto made on Genius indiſcriminately, were only intended as an Introduction to the remarks we propoſe to make in this book on the ſubject of original Genius; to explain the nature, properties, and effects of which, is the principal deſign of this Eſſay.

It may be proper to obſerve, that by the word ORIGINAL, when applied to Genius, we mean that NATIVE and RADICAL power which the mind poſſeſſes, of diſcovering ſomething NEW and UNCOMMON in every ſubject on which it employs its faculties. This power appears in various forms, and operates with various energy, according to its peculiar modification, and the particular degree in which it is beſtowed. Thus it aſ-ſumes, as we have ſeen, a different form, and appears likewiſe in a different degree in the mind of the Philoſopher, from what it doth in that of the Poet or Painter. It is not our preſent buſineſs to inquire what are the proportions and modifications of fancy neceſſary to conſtitute a Genius for particular arts or ſciences, as diſtinguiſhed from each other, ſince this would be an an-

ticipation

ticipation of what is intended to be the ſubject of ſome following Sections. In this we conſider ORIGINAL GENIUS as a GENERAL talent, which may be exerted in any profeſſion, in order to obſerve how happily it is calculated to attain the objects it has in view. We ſhall only farther previouſly remark, that the word ORIGINAL, conſidered in connection with Genius, indicates the DEGREE, not the KIND of this accompliſhment, and that it always denotes its higheſt DEGREE.

Philoſophers have diſtinguiſhed two general ſources of our ideas, from which we draw all our knowledge, SENSATION and REFLECTION. Very different ideas however are excited in the minds of ſome, from thoſe excited in the minds of others, even by the firſt of theſe, which may be ſaid to be the original fountain of our knowledge, though the ideas produced by it are conveyed by organs common to human nature; and ſtill more different ideas are excited in the minds of different perſons by the other faculty, that of REFLECTION. Some perſons indeed have few ideas except ſuch as are derived from ſenſation; they ſeldom ruminate upon, revolve, and compare the impreſſions made upon their minds, unleſs at the time they are made, or while they are recent in their remembrance: hence they become incapable of tracing thoſe relations and analogies which exiſt in nature, but which can only be traced by men of a comprehenſive Imagination and penetrating Judgment. Others, endued with theſe qualities, are rendered thereby capable of aſſociating and disjoining, of comparing and transforming their ideas in ſuch a manner, as to perceive almoſt all their poſſible relations; by which means they are qualified to diſcover the latent truths of ſcience, and to produce the nobleſt monuments of human ingenuity in the ſeveral arts. In other words, they by theſe means become original Geniuſes in that particular art or ſcience, to which they have received the

moſt

most remarkable bias from the hand of Nature.

Original Genius is distinguished from every other degree of this quality, by a more vivid and a more comprehensive Imagination, which enables it both to take in a greater number of objects, and to conceive them more distinctly; at the same time that it can express its ideas in the strongest colours, and represent them in the most striking light. It is likewise distinguished by the superior quickness, as well as justness and extent, of the associating faculty; so that with surprising readiness it combines at once every homogeneous and corresponding idea, in such a manner as to present a complete portrait of the object it attempts to describe. But, above all, it is distinguished by an inventive and plastic Imagination, by which it sketches out a creation of its own, discloses truths that were formerly unknown, and exhibits a succession of scenes and events which were never before contemplated or

con-

conceived. In a word, it is the peculiar character of original Genius to ſtrike out a path for itſelf whatever ſphere it attempts to occupy; to ſtart new ſentiments, and throw out new lights on every ſubject it treats. It delights in every ſpecies of fiction, and ſometimes diſcovers itſelf in the more ſevere inveſtigations of cauſes and effects. It is diſtinguiſhed by the moſt uncommon, as well as the moſt ſurpriſing combinations of ideas; by the novelty, and not unfrequently by the ſublimity and boldneſs of its imagery in compoſition.

Thus much with regard to the nature and characteriſtics of original Genius in general. What we are next to conſider, is its particular and ſingular efficacy in inriching Science with new diſcoveries, and the Arts with new inventions and improvements.

SECTION II.

OF ORIGINAL PHILOSOPHIC GENIUS.

THE empire of Genius is unbounded. All the Sciences and Arts present a ſphere for its exerciſe, and afford ſcope for its exertion. But though it may be exerted indiſcriminately in all, it will not be exerted equally in each. It will ſometimes appear more, ſometimes leſs remarkably. Our preſent inquiry leads us to conſider how and in what degree original Genius will diſplay itſelf in philoſophical Science. In order to perceive this, it may not be improper to conſider the peculiar province of the Philoſopher, and the objects he has in view. His province is to ſurvey with attention

tention the various phenomena of the natural and moral world, and, with perſpicacity of diſcernment, to explore their cauſes; proceeding in his inquiry from the knowledge of effects to the inveſtigation of the cauſes by which they were produced. The objects he has, or ought to have in view, are, to bring into open light thoſe truths that are wrapped in the ſhades of obſcurity, or involved in the mazes of error, and to apply them to the purpoſe of promoting the happineſs of mankind *.

From

* CICERO repreſents it as the peculiar excellence of the *Socratic* Philoſophy, that it had a ſtrict connection with life and manners; and that it was employed on objects of the utmoſt importance to human felicity, on good and evil, on virtue and vice:

Socrates primus Philoſophiam devocavit e cœlo, & in urbibus collocavit, & in domos etiam introduxit, & coegit de vita & moribus, rebusque bonis & malis quærere. *Tuſc. Quæſt.* lib. v. n. 10.

He obſerves, in another part of his Works, that SOCRATES had diſintangled Philoſophy from abſtruſe ſpe-

From this idea of the objects and province of the Philosopher, the intelligent Reader will, upon a little reflection, clearly perceive that vigorous and extensive powers of Imagination are indispensibly necessary to enable him to proceed successfully in the researches of Science. In order however to make this still more evident, let it be observed, that as it is the proper office of this faculty to assemble those ideas, whose relations to the subject it contemplates, and to each other, can alone be determined by the faculty of Judgment; so there are some of these so obvious, that they occur to common

speculations, and applied it to the purposes of common life:

Socrates mihi videtur, id quod constat inter omnes, primus a rebus occultis, & ab ipsa natura involutis, in quibus omnes ante eum philosophi occupati fuerunt, avocavisse philosophiam, & ad vitam communem adduxisse; ut de virtutibus & vitiis omninoque de bonis rebus & malis quæreret; cœlestia autem, vel procul esse a nostra cognitione censeret, vel si maxime cognita essent, nihil tamen ad bene vivendum conferre. *Acad. Quæst.* lib. i. n. 15.

reflec-

reflection, and arise from the general laws of association, while others are so far removed beyond the sphere of the common talents allotted to mankind, that they can neither be assembled nor compared, without such an extraordinary proportion of the powers of Imagination and Reason, as is rarely united in one person. The power of assembling and comparing such ideas, in order to determine their relations and resemblances, is the distinguishing characteristic of an Original Philosophic Genius.

We have formerly observed, that the faculty of the mind, which we distinguish by the name of Imagination, discovers itself in a surprising variety of forms. To create uncommon scenery, to invent new incidents and characters in Poetry, and new theories in Philosophy; to associate and compound, to divide and transform the ideas of the mind, is the work of one and the same power; but is not in all these cases executed with equal ease, or with equal

success,

ſucceſs. To invent and create, muſt undoubtedly require the higheſt exertion of the faculty we are ſpeaking of; becauſe the objects on which the mind employs itſelf in this exerciſe, are very remote from common obſervation, and cannot be brought into view without a ſtrenuous effort of imagination. Hence it happens, that as invention is the province of original Genius, both in Philoſophy and in Poetry, a very great, though not a preciſely equal or ſimilar ſhare of Imagination, is neceſſary in each of them. It will be no incurious employment to obſerve the various exertions of the ſame faculty in theſe different departments, as it will open to us an agreeable proſpect of the ſurpriſing verſatility, extent, and vigour of the human mind; and will alſo enable us to form a comparative idea of the degree of Imagination neceſſary to conſummate original Philoſophic Genius.

The inventive faculty diſplays itſelf in Philoſophy with great force and extent. It

enables

enables the Philoſopher, by its active, vigorous, and exploring power, to conjecture ſhrewdly, if not to comprehend fully, the various ſprings which actuate the viſible ſyſtem of Nature and Providence; to frame the moſt ingenious theories for the ſolution of natural Phenomena; to invent Syſtems, and to new-model the natural and moral World to his own mind. It is intenſely exerciſed in all this proceſs, as it exerts both a creative and combining power; which, by inventing new hypotheſes, by connecting every intermediate and correſponding idea, and by uniting the ſeveral detached parts of one theorem, rears a fabric of its own, whoſe ſymmetry, juſtneſs and ſolidity, it is the buſineſs of the reaſoning faculty to determine.

The kind of Imagination moſt properly adapted to Original Philoſophic Genius, is that which is diſtinguiſhed by REGULARITY, CLEARNESS, and ACCURACY. The kind peculiar to Original Genius in Poetry, is that whoſe

whoſe eſſential properties are a noble IRREGULARITY, VEHEMENCE, and ENTHUSIASM. Or, to ſet the difference betwixt philoſophic and poetic Imagination in another light by the uſe of an image, we may obſerve, that in the mind of the Philoſopher the RAYS of fancy are more COLLECTED, and more CONCENTRATED in one point; and conſequently are more favourable to ACCURATE and DISTINCT VISION: that in the mind of the Poet they are more DIFFUSED; and therefore their luſtre is leſs PIERCING, though more UNIVERSAL. The former perceives the objects he contemplates more CLEARLY; the latter comprehends a greater number of them at ONE GLANCE. Such are the reſpective characters of Imagination in Philoſophy and in Poetry, as diſtinguiſhed from each other.

As we have already obſerved, that an exact equilibrium of the reaſoning and inventive powers of the mind ſeems to be, in a great meaſure, incompatible with their very oppoſite natures, and perhaps was never beſtowed on any individual; the only queſtion is, in what proportion thoſe powers ſhould be diſtributed, in order to the intire conſummation of original philoſophic Genius.

If the poſition we have laid down, and endeavoured to ſupport in a preceding ſection, ſhall be found to be juſt, That Imagination is the diſtinguiſhing ingredient in every kind and degree of Genius, it will obviouſly follow, that this quality muſt predominate in the accompliſhment of original Philoſophic, as well as Poetic Genius. Indeed, with regard to its predominance in the latter, there will be no diſpute. Imagination has by far the greateſt ſhare of merit in poetical productions. It at once deſigns and executes them, calling in only the aſſiſtance of Judgment and Taſte, in order to determine whether it has beſtowed on the ſeveral figures their true proportions, and juſt degrees of light and ſhade. Were we to in-

vert

vert the caſe, and to ſuppoſe Judgment the diſtinguiſhing faculty of the Poet, his productions, it is true, might be more regular and correct; but it is evident, they would be defective in their moſt eſſential excellencies, in FICTION and in FIRE.

With regard to ORIGINAL PHILOSOPHIC GENIUS, it ſeems to be generally imagined, that Judgment is its principal ingredient. As this opinion ſtrikes at the foundation of our theory, it will be neceſſary to examine it with ſome attention.

Let it be obſerved therefore, that as Invention is the peculiar and diſtinguiſhing province of every ſpecies of Genius, Imagination claims an undivided empire over this province. It is this faculty alone, which, without the aid or participation of Judgment, ſupplies all the incidents, characters, imagery, ſentiments, and deſcriptions of Poetry, and moſt of the theories, at leaſt, in Philoſophy; as well as the arguments (a circumſtance not commonly attended to) for ſupporting thoſe theories. Judgment only claims the right of determining their propriety and truth. Since therefore, to ſupply theſe, conſtitutes the higheſt effort of Genius; that faculty which ſupplies them, muſt certainly predominate in its full accompliſhment; and this, we have ſeen, is Imagination. There are at the ſame time inferior degrees of Philoſophic Genius, in which Judgment has the principal aſcendant. Thoſe perſons in whom this diſtribution takes place, are in general qualified for making improvements in Philoſophy, in exact proportion to the degree in which they poſſeſs the talent of Imagination; and will, upon account of the ſuperior ſtrength of their reaſoning talents, be found better qualified for canvaſſing the diſcoveries of others, poſſeſſed of more extenſive powers of Imagination, though perhaps of a leſs penetrating Judgment, than for making thoſe diſcoveries themſelves. It is true indeed, that beſides thoſe philoſophical truths, which, to the

mor-

mortification of the pride of human underſtanding, accident hath brought to light, and thoſe others which have been hit upon by certain happy random thoughts of perſons of very moderate abilities, diſcoveries in Science have ſometimes been made by thoſe, who, enjoying a very ſmall ſhare of imagination, were however endued with a clear apprehenſion, united with a patient and careful obſervation of the various objects they contemplated. It muſt likewiſe be confeſſed, that this method, accompanied with proper experiments, and juſt reaſoning founded on thoſe experiments, though not the moſt expeditious, is however the only certain one of attaining the knowledge of the truths of natural Philoſophy in particular. But then, on the other hand, it muſt be acknowledged, that where an extenſive Imagination is ſuperadded to the qualifications above-mentioned, the mind, being thereby enabled to comprehend a greater variety of objects, and to combine its ideas in a greater variety of forms, becomes qualified to puſh its inquiries much farther, as well as with more advantage.

After all, though Imagination muſt ever be the predominating ingredient in the INTIRE accompliſhment of ORIGINAL PHILOSOPHIC GENIUS, yet the powers of REASON muſt likewiſe exiſt very NEARLY in an equal degree, in order to its COMPLETE conſummation, and the attainment of the objects it has in view; for if we ſhould ſuppoſe Imagination to predominate in a HIGH degree over the other mental faculties, the conſequence would be, that the Philoſopher in whom it thus predominated, would be perpetually employed in forming ingenious indeed, but extravagant theories, of which his compoſitions would take a deep tincture; and we ſhould be amuſed with the DREAMS of a ROMANTIC viſionary, inſtead of being inſtructed in the TRUTHS of SOUND Philoſophy.

Upon

Upon the whole: as both theſe faculties, united in a high degree, muſt concur in forming the truly ORIGINAL PHILOSOPHIC GENIUS, they muſt always go hand in hand together in philoſophical inquiries, as well as exiſt almoſt, though not altogether, in an equal proportion.

Thus we have ſhewn how and by what particular exertions original Genius diſcovers itſelf in Philoſophy; and have pointed out its ſingular efficacy in extending the empire of Science. We have alſo conſidered the kind and degree of Imagination peculiarly adapted to ORIGINAL PHILOSOPHIC GENIUS, compared with the kind and degree of the ſame quality requiſite to ORIGINAL GENIUS in Poetry; at the ſame time that we have ſhewn, that Imagination ought to predominate in the former as well as the latter. We ſhall now conclude this ſection with a few ſlight ſtrictures on the characters of ſome of the moſt diſtinguiſhed original Authors in philosophical Science, by way of illustrating the above remarks.

Of all the Philosophers of antiquity, PLATO possessed the most copious and exuberant imagination, which, joined to a certain contemplative turn of mind, qualified him for the successful pursuit of philosophical studies, and enabled him to acquire an extraordinary eminence in those various branches of Science, to which he applied his divine Genius. He is the only prose writer, who in Philosophy has dared to emulate the sublime majesty of the *Mæonian* Bard †. He was indeed animated with all that ardor and enthusiasm of Imagination which distinguishes the Poet; and it is impossible for a person, possessed of any degree of sensibility, to read his Writings without catching somewhat of the enthusiasm. The

† Παντων δε τουτων μαλιστα ὁ Πλατων, απο του Ομηρικου εκεινου ναματος εις ἀυτον μυριας οσας παρατροπας αποχετευσαμενος. LONG. *de Sub*. cap. 13.

Philosophy

Philoſophy of PLATO, more than that of any other, is calculated to elevate and to expand the ſoul; to ſettle, to ſooth, to refine the paſſions; and to warm the heart with the love of virtue. Such were the objects of this amiable Philoſopher; and ſuch is the tendency of his doctrine. At preſent we conſider his doctrine merely as a proof of his Genius. With this view we may obſerve, that his ſublime contemplations concerning the το ον and the το ἓν *, the exiſtence

* Thoſe who are deſirous to know PLATO's ſentiments on the exiſtence and unity of the Divine Nature, may conſult his *Philebus*, the fifth and ſixth books of his *Republic*, and his *Parmenides*; in all which they will find the reaſoning very ſubtile; and in ſome places, particularly through moſt of the laſt mentioned dialogue, it muſt be confeſſed, very intricate. For this reaſon, we chooſe rather to refer the Reader to thoſe parts of PLATO's Works, where his ſentiments on the above-mentioned ſubjects are contained, than to preſent him with a few detached paſſages, which could convey no diſtinct idea of his meaning, where the chain of argumentation is ſo ſtrictly connected. We ſhall only obſerve, that though PLATO ſometimes ſpeaks

ence and unity of the ſupreme Being, as well as the † perfections and providence of

---

ſpeaks agreeably to the eſtabliſhed mythology of his country, yet when he intends to deliver his genuine ſentiments, he maintains the abſolute Sovereignty and Unity of the Deity.

† PLATO, in his *Politicus*, after delivering an ingenious, however unphiloſophical a theory, concerning the various transformations and revolutions the world had undergone; and after having repreſented it as decayed and worn out in the courſe of ſo many tranſmutations, as well as in danger of immediate diſſolution, upon account of the diſorder into which its different parts had been thrown, deſcribes the Deity, with great ſublimity, as riſing from his ſeat of contemplation, reſuming the reins of government, preſiding at the helm, arranging the disjointed parts of the vaſt machine of the world, reſtoring them to their primitive order and beauty, and beſtowing upon the whole renewed vigour and immortality. As this paſſage gives a noble idea of the omnipotence of the Deity, we ſhall preſent the Reader with it.

Διο δη και τοτ' ηδη θεος ὁ κοσμησας αυτον, καθορων εν αποριαις οντα, κηδομενος ἵνα μη χειμασθεις, υπο ταραχης διαλυθεις, εις τον της ανομοιοτητος απειρον οντα τοπον δυη παλιν εφεδρος αυτω των πηδαλιων γιγνομενος, τα νοσησαντα και λυθεντα εν τη καθ' αυτον

of the Deity; that his theory concerning the cauſes, firſt principles, and generation of

αὐτον προτερα περιοδῳ ςρεψας, κοσμει τε και επανορθων, αθανατον αυτον και αγηρω απεργαζεται. Edit. *Mars. Ficin.* p. 538.

Our Philoſopher, expreſſing his own opinion, by the mouth of the *Ælian* Gueſt, attributes the creation of all things, even of the materials of which he ſuppoſes the animal world to be framed, to one ſupreme Being:

Ημεις μεν που και τ' αλλα ζωα, και εξ ὧν τα πεφυκοτ' εςι, πυρ και υδωρ και τα τουτων αδελφα, θεου γεννηματα τα παντα, ισμεν αυτα απειργασμενα εκαςα? *Soph.* p. 185.

At the end of his *Timæus*, he repreſents the world as the intelligent, moſt perfect image of the Deity:

Θνητα γαρ και αθανατα ζωα λαβων, και ξυμπληρωθεις ὅδε ὁ κοσμος, ὅυτω ζωον ορατον, τα ορατα περιεχον, εικων του νοητου θεου, αισθητος, μεγιςος και αριςος καλλιςος τε και τελεωτατος γεγονεν, εἱς ουρανος ὅδε, μονογενης ων. *Tim.* p. 1089.

And in the ſame dialogue he lays it down as an indiſputable maxim, that God made all things perfect in their kind:

Το δε ἡ δυνατον ὡς καλλιςα τε και αριςα εξ ουχ ουτως εχοντων, τον θεον αυτα ξυνιςαναι περι παντα ημιν ως αει τουτο λεγομενον υπαρχετω. p. 1062.

of things, and the ſoul which animates and actuates the whole frame of Nature *; his ſentiments concerning virtue,

---

In other paſſages, PLATO celebrates the moral as well as natural perfections of the Deity. Thus he repreſents him as the complete model of juſtice.

Θεος ουδαμη ουδαμως αδικος, αλλ ὡς οιον τε δικαιοτατος. και ουκ εστιν αυτω ὁμοιοτερον ουδεν η ὁς αν ημων αυ γενηται ὅ τι δικαιοτατος. *Theæt.* p. 129.

He makes SOCRATES likewiſe ſtrongly aſſert the doctrine of a particular Providence, exerciſed in favour of good men. This laſt, addreſſing himſelf to ſuch of his judges as had vindicated his innocence, makes the following declaration:

Αλλα και υμεις χρη ω ανδρες δικασται, ευελπιδας ειναι προς τον θανατον. και εν τι τουτο διανοεισθαι, αληθες ὁτι ουκ εστι ανδρι αγαθω κακον ουδεν ουτε ζῶντι, ουτε τελευτησαντι. *Apoll. Socrat.* p. 31.

* PLATO's doctrines concerning the *Anima Mundi*, the Soul of the World, the cauſes, original principles, and formation of things, the revolutions of matter, and tranſmigration of ſouls, are among the profound myſteries of his Philoſophy. Speaking of the *Anima Mundi*, as infuſed by the Deity, he tells us;

ture *; and the happineſs of thoſe ſouls who are gradually appropriated to the ſo-

Ψυχην δε εις το μεσον αυτȣ θεις, δια παντος τε ετεινε, και ετι εξω το σωμα αυτη περιεκαλυψε, και κυκλω δη κυκλον ϛρεφομενον, ουρανον ἕνα μονον ερημον κατεϛησε. *Tim.* p. 1049.

Thoſe who are deſirous of obtaining full ſatisfaction on this and the above-mentioned ſubjects, may conſult the *Timæus*, where they will find them particularly treated; and where they will be entertained with a variety of notions ſtrangely fanciful, indicating the inexhauſtible fecundity of Imagination peculiar to this great Philoſopher.

* Plato conſiders virtue in ſeveral different lights; ſubſtituting ſome of its particular and eſſential ingredients in place of the general quality which they conſtitute. Thus he ſubſtitutes juſtice at one time for this quality, at another, temperance, at another, fortitude; but poſitively maintains that it cannot be taught, but muſt be implanted in the mind by divine fate; an opinion which gives us a very ſublime idea of the nature of virtue:

Ει δε νυν ἡμεις εν παντι τω λογω τουτω καλως εζητησαμεν τε και ελεγομεν, αρετη αν ειη ουτε φυσει, ουτε διδακτον· αλλα θεια μοιρα παραγιγνομενη ανευ νου, οις αν παρα γιγνηται. *Meno*, p. 427.

vereign

vereign good and the supreme beauty †; that his reflections on prayer *, and on divine

---

† In speaking of the sovereign good and supreme beauty, he breaks out into a kind of divine enthusiasm, which absorbs his mental faculties in rapturous admiration and love of that glorious Object, which his ardent Imagination had represented as inexpressibly amiable:

Τι δητα (εφη) οιομεθα, ειτω γενοιτο αυτο το καλον ιδειν ειλικρινες, καθαρον, αμικτον, αλλ' ἁ μη αναπλεων σαρκων τε ανθρωπινων και χρωματων, και αλλης πολλης φλυαριας θνητης, αλλ' αυτο το θειον, καλον δυναιτο μονοειδες κατιδειν; αρ' οιει (εφη) φαυλον βιον γιγνεσθαι εκεισε βλεποντος ανθρωπου, και εκεινο ὁ δει θεωμενου και ξυνοντος αυτω; η ουκ ενθυμη (εφη) ὁτι ινταυθα αυτω μοναχου γενησεται, ορωντι ᾧ ορατον το καλον, τικτειν ουκ ειδωλα αρετης ἁτε ουκ ειδωλου εφαπτομενω; αλλ' αληθη, ἁτε του αληθους εφαπτομενω; τεκοντι δε αρετην αληθη, και θρεψαμενω, υπαρχει θεοφιλει γενεσθαι, και ειπερ τω αλλω ανθρωπω, αθανατω και εκεινω. *Sympos.* p. 1199.

* It is pretty generally known, that the nature and qualifications of the duty of prayer, compose the subject of the second Alcibiades. Socrates, having convinced this young hero of the absurdity, as well as impiety of addressing the Gods rashly, recommends that form of prayer used by a certain Poet:

Ζευ

vine love and friendſhip †, are ſtriking inſtances of the fertility of our Philoſopher's imagination,

Ζευ βασιλευ, τα μεν εσθλα και ευχομενοις και ανευκτοις
Αμμι διδε, τα δε δεινα και ευχομενοις απαλεξειν κελευει.

P. 454.

Having impreſſed upon the mind of ALCIBIADES a deep ſenſe of the importance of the duty of prayer, in which he was going to engage, and at the ſame time ſhewn him how apt moſt men were, from their ignorance of what was really good for them, to aſk from the Gods, what, if granted, might prove highly deſtructive to themſelves; he obſerves, that it becomes us to conſider well, before we addreſs thoſe ſuperior Beings, what we ought, and what we ought not to ſay:

Αλλα δοκει μοι πολλης φυλακης δεισθαι και σκεψεως, ὅ, τι ποτε ῥητεον εςι και μη. P. 458.

And a little after, from the conſideration of our own ignorance, he infers the neceſſity of waiting for divine Illumination, in order to enable us to perform the duty of prayer properly:

Αναγκαιον ουν εςι περιμενειν εως αν τις μαθῃ ως δει προς θεους και προς ανθρωπους διακεισθαι.

† In the dialogue, intitled *Lyſis*, PLATO gives us the opinion of his Maſter concerning the nature of friendſhip.

imagination, as well as of that moral and ſpeculative diſpoſition, which we have elſewhere obſerved to diſtinguiſh Philoſophic Genius *.

It will perhaps be alledged, that the moſt ſublime notions in PLATO's Philoſophy were originally derived from divine revelation, and that he had little elſe than the merit of collecting and forming them into a ſyſtem. This point GALE, in his *Court of the Gentiles*,

ſhip. SOCRATES, intending to reclaim the unhappy youth from whom the dialogue takes its name, from thoſe criminal indulgences into which he was in hazard of being betrayed, leads him, ſtep by ſtep, from the means to the end, from the conſideration of inferior enjoyments to the contemplation of the SOVEREIGN, ULTIMATE, and UNCREATED GOOD, in which all ſubordinate gratifications ought to center, and on which our moſt ardent affections ought to be fixed:

Αρ ȣν ȣκ αναγκη απειπειν ημας ὁυτως ιοντας; και αφικεσθαι επι τινα αρχην, ἡ ȣκ επανοισει επ' αλλο φιλον, αλλ' ἡξει επ' εκεινο ὁ εςι πρωτον φιλον. ὁυ ενεκα και τα αλλα φαμεν παντα φιλα ειναι. *Lyſis*, p. 507.

* Book I. Sect. 2.

hath

hath laboured to prove. It muſt indeed be confeſſed, that PLATO enjoyed great advantages, and was favoured with peculiar means and opportunities of acquiring knowledge, which he did not fail to improve. Having travelled into *Egypt* and *Italy*, he made himſelf acquainted with the myſteries of the *Egyptian* Prieſts, as well as with the more ſecret and profound doctrines of the *Pythagorean* School ;. and no doubt by tradition, however corrupted and interpolated, he might obtain ſome very imperfect knowledge of the fundamental principles of the Jewiſh religion. Indeed the ſtrong reſemblance betwixt the doctrines of PLATO, and thoſe contained in the Old Teſtament, renders this conjecture highly probable. At the ſame time it appears equally probable, that as others are very different both from the Sacred and *Pythagorean* doctrines, they are properly derived from neither, but are the production of his own inventive Genius.

Des Cartes, the *French* Philoſopher, had the honour of firſt reforming the Philoſophy of his country. He ſtruck out a path for himſelf, through the gloom which the obſcure and unintelligible jargon of the Schools had thrown on Science; and though he could not purſue it through its ſeveral windings, he pointed out the track which has been followed by others, and has led to the moſt important diſcoveries. He inherited from nature a ſtrong and vivid Imagination; but the too great predominance and indulgence of this very faculty, was the cauſe of all thoſe errors in Philoſophy into which he was betrayed. His theories of the different vortices of the heavenly bodies, and of that immenſe whirlpool of fluid matter, through which, in conſequence of an original impulſe, they are ſuppoſed to revolve, have, by our celebrated Newton, been ſhewn to be falſe; though thoſe theories are a proof of the creative Imagination of their Author; but of an imagination too freely indulged, and too little ſub-

ſubjected to the prudent reſtraints of Judgment.

What DES CARTES was to the *French*, Lord BACON was to the *Engliſh* nation. He was indeed not only the reformer, but the reviver and reſtorer of Learning. As his penetrating and comprehenſive Genius * enabled

* Perhaps no age or nation can boaſt of having produced a more comprehenſive and univerſal Genius, than that which Lord BACON ſeems to have poſſeſſed. He applied his Genius to almoſt every department of Literature and Science, and ſucceeded in every ſphere which he attempted. Human knowledge was divided by him into three diſtinct branches, Hiſtory, Poetry, and Philoſophy (vid. *de Aug. Scient.* ſect. 1.) the firſt relating to the Memory, the ſecond to the Imagination, and the laſt to Reaſon or the Judgment. With reſpect to Philoſophy, inſtead of employing his imagination in framing air-built theories, he began his inquiries into the works of nature, with laying it down as a fundamental maxim, that man knows juſt as much only of the courſe of nature, as he has learned from obſervation and experience: "Homo naturæ miniſter & interpres, "tantum facit & intelligit, quantum de naturæ ordine, "re vel mente obſervaverit, nec amplius ſcit aut poteſt,"

enabled him to difcern and expofe the errors of the Scholaftic Philofophy; fo it qualified him not only for extending the empire of Science far beyond the limits within which it had been formerly confined, but alfo for difcovering thofe immenfe tracts of uncultivated ground, which fince his time, by tracing his footfteps, have been occupied and improved. He had the honour of introducing experimental Philofophy *, and fucceeded

---

(*Nov. Org.* lib. i. aph. 1.) and upon this juft axiom, the refult of mature reflection and good fenfe, he founded all his philofophical difcoveries.

* When we affirm that Lord BACON introduced experimental Philofophy into his country, we do not mean to affert, that its ufe was wholly unknown before his time; but that he was the firft who taught and regularly practifed the method of inveftigating the caufes of the phenomena of nature by certain experiments. The excellence and advantage of this method of inveftigation he celebrates very juftly: "Sed demonftratio "longe optima eft *experientia*; modo hæreat in ipfo "*experimento*. Nam fi traducatur ad alia quæ *fimilia* "exiftimantur, nifi *rite* & *ordine* fiat illa tractatio res "*fallax* eft." (*Ibid.* fect. 70.) After which he cenfures

ceeded in many of the experiments which he made. Thofe particularly, in which, by the help of a pneumatic engine he had himfelf contrived, he endeavoured to difcover the weight and elafticity of the air, in which he was to a great degree fuccefsful, though the above-mentioned properties were more minutely calculated afterwards, do abundance of credit to his philofophical fagacity. His moral Effays, his book *de Augmentis Scientiarum* *, his

fures the *partial*, *inaccurate*, and *cafual* method of making experiments in his own time; in oppofition to which he points out the true procefs to be obferved by the Philofopher, who afpires to the honour of extending the limits of human knowledge: "At contra verus "experientiæ ordo primum lumen accendit, deinde "per lumen iter demonftrat, incipiendo ab experien-"tia ordinata & digefta, & minime præpoftera aut er-"ratica, atque ex ea educendo axiomata, atque ex "axiomatibus conftitutis rurfus experimenta nova." (*Ibid.*)

* The defign of the book *de Augmentis Scientiarum*, is to take a general furvey of human knowledge, divide it into its feveral branches, obferve the deficiencies in thofe branches, and fuggeft the methods by which

his *Novum Organum* †, and his treatises of Physics and Natural History ‡, have gained him great reputation; as indeed all his works are a proof of his having possessed that nice

---

which they may be supplied; an undertaking executed in a great measure by the Author himself in some following tracts.

† In the *Novum Organum Scientiarum*, the Author points out the causes of ignorance and error in the Sciences, at the same time that he lays down certain aphorisms, founded on perception and consciousness, or deduced from observation and experience, as so many steps in the intellectual scale, by which we may rise to the knowledge of universal truths. Those leading disquisitions and experiments are likewise pointed out, which open to us the most comprehensive views of the works of nature, as well as facilitate the inventions and improvements of the arts.

‡ The Author, in his *Sylva Sylvarum*, attempts a kind of history of nature and art; enumerates many of the phenomena of the universe for this purpose, which he calls the third part of his Instauration; and in the fourth part of this Work, denominated *Scala Intellectus*, he shews the method of employing the materials of the *Sylva Sylvarum*, by a variety of examples, such as his History of Life and Death, his History of the Winds, and his Condensation and Rarefaction of natural Bodies.

tem-

temperature of Imagination and Judgment, which conſtitute truly original Philoſophic Genius.

In adducing examples of this quality, it would be inexcuſable to omit mentioning Sir Isaac Newton, a name ſo revered by Mathematicians and Philoſophers of every degree. This great man was doubtleſs in Philoſophy an original Genius of the firſt rank. His various and ſtupendous diſcoveries of the revolutions of the heavenly bodies, as well as of the laws by which thoſe revolutions are regulated; of their ſeveral magnitudes, orbits, and diſtances; and of that great and fundamental law of attraction, by which all nature is ſupported and actuated; his theory of light, as an emanation from the ſun; his calculation of its rapidity, and of the reflection and refrangibility of its rays; his ſubtil and curious anatomy of thoſe rays, and the diviſion and arrangement of the elementary ones which compoſe them, together with their union in the formation of colours, are the moſt aſtoniſhing efforts of the human mind; and while they ſhew the prodigious compaſs of that imagination, which could frame and comprenend ſuch ſublime conceptions, they at the ſame time clearly evince the profound depth of penetration and ſtrength of reaſon, which, by a kind of divine intuition, could diſcern and demonſtrate their truth.

Doctor BERKELEY, Biſhop of *Cloyne*, was another original philoſophic Genius of diſtinguiſhed eminence. While HOBBES and SPINOZA maintained the doctrine of abſolute materialiſm, admitting nothing but matter, in one form or another, in the univerſe, BERKELEY excluded it altogether from his ſyſtem, and denied its exiſtence out of a mind perceiving it. A doctrine ſo new and uncommon, and ſeemingly ſo contrary to the evidence of our ſenſes, could not fail at firſt to raiſe aſtoniſhment, and to meet with oppoſition: yet this ingenious Author has ſupported his theory by ſuch plauſible arguments,

ments, that many perſons appear to be convinced by them, and to have adopted his ſentiments. The truth is, though, relying on the teſtimony of our ſenſes, we allow the real exiſtence of matter, and are ſufficiently acquainted with its eſſential properties, ſolidity, extenſion, and diviſibility; yet its genuine eſſence, or the ſubſtratum in which thoſe properties exiſt, is ſtill a myſtery to Philoſophers, and will probably continue to be ſo. Whether the above-mentioned tenet of this Author ſhould be generally received as an eſtabliſhed article in the Philoſopher's Creed, or not, it muſt, ſupported as it is with ſuch ſtrength of reaſon and invention, undoubtedly be conſidered as a ſignal proof of his having poſſeſſed a very high degree of original Philoſophic Genius.

The laſt original Genius in Philoſophy, we ſhall take notice of, is BURNET, the Author of *the Theory of the Earth*; a ſyſtem ſo new, ſo conſiſtent, and conceived with ſuch ſtrength of fancy, that one is almoſt tempted

to

to be of the ſame opinion with the Author of *the Eſſay on the Writings and Genius of* POPE, who hath ventured to declare, that in this admirable performance, there appears a degree of Imagination little inferior to what is diſcovered in *Paradiſe Loſt*. His hypotheſes of the poſition and form of the antediluvian earth, of the cauſes which produced the univerſal deluge, occaſioned by the opening of the floodgates of Heaven, aided by the burſting aſunder of the frame of the earth, and its falling into the great abyſs, with which it was ſurrounded, and on which it as it were floated; his opinions of the paradiſiacal ſtate, of the agreeable temperature of its ſeaſons, and of the peculiar beauties of this primeval conſtitution of nature; his theory of the general conflagration, its cauſes and progreſs, and of the univerſal judgment conſequent upon it, together with his idea of the nature, happineſs, and time of the Millenium, form altogether ſuch a ſurpriſing, ingenious, and at the ſame time, not improbable ſyſtem, that we cannot help ad-

miring

miring the whole as the production of an inventive and truly creative Genius.

These examples, we hope, will be sufficient to shew the importance, the use, and the sphere of Imagination in philosophical disquisitions; and to point out those particular degrees, and that happy temperature of Imagination and Judgment, which constitute and accomplish original Philosophic Genius. Many other distinguished names in Philosophy might have been added to those abovementioned; but as the narrow limits of our plan, on this branch of the subject, do not allow our running out to greater length in the way of illustration, so the adducing more examples, in order to confirm the preceding remarks, will, we imagine, after those already adduced, be altogether unnecessary.

SECTION III.

OF ORIGINAL GENIUS IN POETRY.

POETRY *, of all the liberal Arts, affords the moſt extenſive ſcope for the

---

* ARISTOTLE, inquiring into the origin of Poetry, aſſigns two principal cauſes of it, a natural DESIRE of IMITATION, and the pleaſure ariſing from the ſucceſs of that IMITATION:

Εοικασι δε γεννησαι μεν ὁλως την ποιητικην αιτιαι δυο τινες, και ἁυται φυσικαι. Το, τε γαρ μιμεισθαι, συμφυτον τοις ανθρωποις εκ παιδων εϛι, και τȣτω διαφερȣσι των αλλων ζωων, οτι μιμη-

the diſplay of a Genius truly Original. In Philoſophy, the empire of Imagination, and conſequently of Genius, is in ſome degree neceſſarily reſtricted; in Poetry, it is altogether abſolute and unconfined. To accompliſh the Philoſopher, who would make new diſcoveries in Science, a large proportion of Imagination is (as we have already ſhewn) undoubtedly requiſite; but to conſtitute the true Poet, the higheſt degree of this quality is indiſpenſibly neceſſary. Smooth verſification and harmonious numbers will no more make genuine Poetry, than the atoms of a ſkeleton put together can make an animated and living figure. To produce either, a certain vital ſpirit muſt be infuſed; and in Poetry, this vital ſpirit is INVENTION †. By this

μιμητικωτατον εστι, και τας μαθησεις ποιειται δια μιμησεως τας πρωτας, και το χαιρειν τοις μιμημασι παντας. *Ariſt. Poet.* cap. 4.

† The ſame great Critic obſerves, that as it is the office of the Hiſtorian to relate ſuch things as are really done, it is the proper office of the Poet to relate the kind

this quality it is principally characterised; which, being the very soul of all poetical composition, is likewise the source of that inchanting delight, which the mind receives from its perusal. Invention may be considered as consisting of INCIDENTS, of CHARACTERS, of IMAGERY, of SENTIMENT; in all which, original poetic Genius will display itself in an uncommon degree. We shall consider its efforts in each of these separately.

---

kind of things that should be done, according to what is required by necessity, or the rules of probability:

Φανερον δε εκ των ειρημενων, και οτι ου το τα γινομενα λεγειν, τουτο ποιητου εργον εστιν, αλλ᾽ οια αν γενοιτο, και τα δυνατα κατα το εικος, η το αναγκαιον. Ὁ γαρ ἱστορικος και ὁ ποιητης, ου τω η εμμετρα λεγειν η αμετρα διαφερουσιν· ειη γαρ αν τα Ἡροδοτου εις μετρα τιθεναι, και ουδεν ηττον αν ειη ἱστορια τις μετα μετρου η ανευ μετρων· αλλα τουτω διαφερει τω τον μεν τα γινομενα λεγειν, τον δε οια αν γενοιτο. *Ibid.* cap. 9.

In order however to relate the kind of things that should be done, the Poet must possess the power of Invention.

First,

First, in the invention of INCIDENTS. Some incidents are so obvious, that by a natural association of ideas, they instantly occur to the mind of every one possessed of ordinary abilities, and are very easily conceived. Others however are more remote, and lie far beyond the reach of ordinary faculties *; coming only within the verge of those

* A person who is destitute of Imagination, must necessarily regard a series of fictitious incidents, which are at the same time surprising and important, with great astonishment; and he will feel it extremely difficult to conceive them to have been invented by the mere fertility of the Poet's fancy. The reason of both seems to be this: Such a person, having scarce any other ideas than what arise from sensation, and the most common laws of association, will be apt to suppose that all mankind receive their ideas by the same modes of conveyance; being ignorant of those exquisitely nice relations of ideas resulting from certain laws of combination that do not operate upon his own mind, but which, operating upon minds of a finer frame, are the source of that rich fund of Invention which he admires, but can scarce comprehend. Sensation and reflection are indeed the common fountains of all our ideas and all our knowledge; but when once those ideas are conveyed into the mind by means of the senses,

those few persons, whose minds are capacious enough to contain that prodigious croud of ideas, which an extensive observation and experience supply; whose understandings are penetrating enough to discover the most distant connections of those ideas, and whose imaginations are sufficiently quick, in combining them at pleasure. It is this kind of incidents which original Genius delights to invent; incidents which are in themselves great as well as uncommon. Let it not however be supposed, that the invention even of these is a laborious employment to a Writer of this stamp; for it is the prerogative of a great Genius to think and to write with ease, very rarely, if ever, expe-

senses, they undergo an infinite variety of modification in the mind of a man of Genius, in comparison of what they admit of in one who is destitute of this quality. In the former case, Imagination, like a grand alembic, gradually refines, and (if I may use the expression) sublimates those conceptions that heretofore participated of the grossness of sense, from which they were ultimately derived.

riencing

riencing a barrenneſs of Imagination. He has nothing to do but to give ſcope to the excurſions of this faculty, which, by its active and creative power, exploring every receſs of thought, will ſupply an inexhauſtible variety of ſtriking incidents. A facility, therefore, of inventing and combining ſuch incidents in compoſition, may be regarded as one characteriſtical indication of a Genius truly Original *.

The

* It is, we believe, commonly ſuppoſed, at leaſt it ſeems to be the opinion of ſome, that the invention of a variety of new and intereſting incidents, is the moſt ſignal proof and exertion of Genius. This opinion, however, though, upon the firſt reflection it has an air of probability, will appear, upon a ſtricter inquiry, to be without any foundation. The invention of characters, which will be afterwards particularly conſidered, is unqueſtionably the greateſt effort of original Genius. In ſupport of this poſition, let it be obſerved, that in this ſpecies of Invention, the mind has a greater diverſity of objects to employ it; and muſt therefore, in order to comprehend them, exert its faculties with vigour, as well as keep them on the ſtretch. Thus, in the exhibition of an uncommon character, the Imagination muſt invent the SENTIMENTS, LANGUAGE,

 MANNERS,

The second species of invention we mentioned was that of CHARACTERS. Ordinary

---

MANNERS, and OFFICES peculiar to it, and Judgment must determine concerning the PROPRIETY of each; in the execution of which it is evident, both these faculties must be very INTENSELY exercised, particularly the first; since to conceive and represent characters which never existed, but are the pure CREATION of the mind (for of such only we are speaking at present) must indicate the utmost FERTILITY and FORCE of Imagination. On the other hand, though we readily allow the invention of various, important, and surprising events, to be a proof of the existence of original Genius in a high degree, yet we cannot regard it as so remarkable an exertion of this talent, as the invention of uncommon characters; because the imagination of an original Author in Poetry, feeling a native bent to fiction, will, even in its pastime, naturally run into the first, as incidents are less COMPLICATED, and therefore more easily invented than characters; but it cannot accomplish the last without the most strenuous efforts. Were we to admit the invention of surprising incidents, as the most distinguishing criterion of ORIGINALITY, we should be under a necessity of assigning the superiority in this respect to ARIOSTO, over HOMER and SHAKESPEAR; since we find that a much greater variety of events have been feigned in the *Orlando Furioso* of the former, than in all

nary Writers, and even thoſe who are poſſeſſed of no inconſiderable talents, commonly ſatisfy themſelves, in this branch of compoſition, with copying the characters which have been drawn by Authors of ſuperior merit, and think they acquit themſelves ſufficiently, when they produce a juſt reſemblance of the originals they profeſs to imitate. A moderate degree of praiſe is no doubt due to ſucceſsful imitators; but an Author of original Genius will not content himſelf with a mediocrity of reputation; conſcious of the ſtrength of his own talents, he diſdains to imitate what perhaps he is qualified to excel. Imitation indeed, of every kind, except that of nature, has a tendency to cramp the inventive powers of the mind, which, if indulged in their excurſions, might diſcover new mines of intellectual

all the Works of the two laſt mentioned Poets put together; a preference ſurely, which neither the dictates of impartial Reaſon, nor the laws of ſound Criticiſm, could ever juſtify.

ore, that lie hid only from those who are incapable or unwilling to dive into the recesses in which it lies buried. A Writer however, of the kind last mentioned, instead of tracing the footsteps of his predecessors, will allow his imagination to range over the field of Invention, in quest of its materials; and, from the group of figures collected by it, will strike out a character like his own Genius, perfectly Original.

It may be observed, that there are three different kinds of characters, in the invention and representation of which, originality of Genius may be discovered with GREAT, though not with EQUAL advantage. The first of these are real human characters, such as are found in every country and age. The second are likewise human, but of the most dignified kind; raised far above the level of common life, and peculiar to the purest and most heroic times. The last sort of characters is that of beings wholly different in their natures from mankind; such as Ghosts,

Witches,

Witches, Fairies, and the like, which may be termed ſupernatural.

Perhaps it may be thought, that in the firſt of theſe caſes, Invention has nothing to do, and cannot with any propriety be exerciſed; ſince to conceive juſtly, and to expreſs naturally, are the principal requiſites in an Author, who would exhibit a faithful portrait of real characters. It muſt be confeſſed, that in this inſtance there is not ſo much ſcope afforded for invention as in the others; nay farther, that it is neceſſarily much reſtricted. But let it be obſerved, that though juſt and lively conceptions of the characters to be repreſented, together with the power of deſcribing thoſe conceptions, are the qualifications moſt eſſentially requiſite to the faithful exhibition of ſuch characters, both theſe qualities depend upon the Imagination; for though impartial Judgment muſt determine how far the intire reſemblance is juſt, yet to dictate the ſentiments and language, and to furniſh the actions peculiar to the different perſons exhibited, is the work of Invention alone. It will be readily underſtood, that we are at preſent ſpeaking of characters repreſented on the ſtage, and taken from real life, in the deſcribing of which we ſuppoſe an original Author to employ his Genius †.

The

† It cannot be doubted but that Original Genius may be diſcovered in Comedy and works of Humour, as well as in the higher ſpecies of Poetry, thoſe of Tragedy and the *Epopœa*; though the originality diſcovered in the firſt will be very different, both in kind and degree, from that which is diſcovered in the two laſt.

Thus the Author of *Hudibras* was in his peculiar way an Original, as well as the Author of the *Iliad*; and HOGARTH, in drawing ſcenes and characters in low life, with ſuch uncommon propriety, juſtneſs and humour, diſcovers a certain ORIGINALITY, though far inferior IN ITS KIND to what appears in thoſe illuſtrious monuments of Genius left us by RAPHAEL URBIN and MICHAEL ANGELO. There can be no queſtion which of the Poets, or which of the Painters, was the greateſt Genius; for the comparative merit of illuſtrious or ingenious Artiſts is eſtimated, not merely from the EXECUTION, but from the DESIGN, and from the SUBJECT which employed their pens and pencils. Thus there is a ſub-

The ſecond ſort of characters, in the invention and proper repreſentation of which we

---

a ſublimity in the works of the Epic Bard, and in the pieces of the Hiſtory Painters above-mentioned, which gives them a vaſt ſuperiority over thoſe of the humorous Poet and ludicrous Artiſt already named.

We obſerved likewiſe, that the DEGREE of ORIGINALITY which may be diſcovered in the higher ſpecies of Poetry, is different from that which Comedy admits of. The DEGREE of ORIGINALITY in any performance whatever, depends upon the degree of INVENTION appearing in it; and as there is in general at leaſt occaſion for a greater proportion of this quality in Tragedy and the *Epopœa*, than in Comedy, we may infer, that a greater degree of ORIGINAL GENIUS is requiſite to an excellence in the two firſt, than is neceſſary to an excellence in the laſt. In the former, both the characters and incidents are in a great meaſure FICTITIOUS; in the latter, they are for the moſt part taken from REAL life; the one ſetting before our eyes an illuſtrious model of virtue, teaches us what we SHOULD BE; the other preſenting to our view a faithful portrait of our vices and follies, drawn from obſervation, teaches us what WE ARE. Hence it ſhould ſeem, that a SUBLIME and CREATIVE Imagination is neceſſary to conſtitute a TALENT for Epic Poetry, or for Tragedy; and that a QUICK and LIVELY one, ac-we obſerved an original Genius would excel, is that of the moſt elevated kind, ſuch as is raiſed far above the ordinary ſtandard of human excellence, yet not altogether above the ſphere of humanity; ſuch as is not abſolutely unattainable by man, but is rarely found in common life, and is peculiar to the moſt heroic ages of the world. It is this kind of characters which is moſt ſuitable to the dignity of the epic and the tragic Muſe: the latter indeed hath greatly extended her prerogative, by aſſuming the privilege of repreſenting every kind of diſtreſs, and making vicious characters frequently the principal perſonages of the drama. We ſhall only by the way obſerve on this ſubject, that though one end of Tragedy, the exciting of terror, may be anſwered moſt effectually by this method, the other ends, namely, the raiſing of our admiration and pity, can by no means

companied with an extenſive KNOWLEDGE of mankind, is the principal requiſite to a MASTERY in Comedy.

be

be accomplished by it; since to effectuate these, virtue must appear great and venerable in distress. Though virtuous characters labouring under calamities, do at least in general afford the most proper subjects for Tragedy, as appears from the reason already given, yet we are far from laying it down as an essential rule, that such characters must always be exhibited in this branch of Poetry; for we are sensible, that as Tragedy admits of great latitude with regard to the choice of its subjects, it is a rule which may sometimes with propriety be transgressed; yet we will lay it down as an inviolable law in the conduct of an Epic Poem, that the characters of the principal persons must be virtuous and illustrious. In representing characters of this kind, whether in Tragedy or the *Epopœa*, an original Genius will discover the fertility and richness of his invention. Finding no characters in real life every way suited to his purpose, his Imagination amply supplies the defect, and enables him to form those complete models of excellence, which neither

neither obſervation nor experience could furniſh. By the creative and combining power of this faculty, he aſſembles thoſe ſhining qualities which conſtitute the Hero, and exhibits them, united together with perfect ſymmetry, in one ſtriking and graceful figure. Inſtead of copying the Heroes of HOMER, or of any other Author ancient or modern, he will preſent us with Heroes which are properly his own; being the tranſcripts of thoſe models of genuine excellence, which he has formed in his own mind. We do not affirm that ſuch characters will be altogether imaginary. The groundwork may be taken from hiſtory or tradition, though it is the province of the Poet to finiſh the piece; and the Poet that is truly original, will do this with admirable art and invention.

The third and laſt ſort of characters, in which, above all others, an original Genius will moſt remarkably diſplay his invention, is of that kind which we called PRETERNA-

TURAL,

TURAL, and is altogether different from mere HUMAN charaĉters. Witches, Ghoſts, Fairies, and ſuch other unknown viſionary beings, are included in the ſpecies of which we are ſpeaking. Of the manner of exiſt-ence, nature and employment of theſe won-derful beings, we have no certain or deter-minate ideas. It ſhould ſeem that our no-tions of them, vague and indiſtinĉt as they are, are derived from tradition and popular opinion; or are the children of Fancy, Su-perſtition, and Fear. Theſe cauſes concur-ing with, as well as operating upon, the natural credulity of mankind, have given birth to prodigies and fables concerning "Gorgons, and Hydras, and chimeras dire;" which have been always eagerly ſwallowed by the vulgar, though they may have been juſtly rejeĉted by the wiſe. However averſe the latter may be to think with the former on ſubjeĉts of this kind, it is certain, that their ideas of Ghoſts, Witches, Dæmons, and ſuch like appari-tions, muſt be very much the ſame with theirs,

theirs, ſince they draw them from the ſame ſource, that of traditionary relation; and how reluctant ſoever the Judgment may be to yield its aſſent, the Imagination catches and retains the impreſſion, whether we will or not. It is true, the ideas of thoſe beings, which are common to all, are very general and obſcure; there is therefore great ſcope afforded for the flights of Fancy in this boundleſs region. Much may be invented, and many new ideas of their nature and offices may be acquired. The wildeſt and moſt exuberant imagination will ſucceed beſt in excurſions of this kind, "beyond the viſible diurnal ſphere," and will make the moſt ſtupendous diſcoveries in its aerial tour. In this region of fiction and fable, original Genius will indulge its adventurous flight without reſtraint: it will dart a beam upon the dark ſcenes of futurity, draw the veil from the inviſible world, and expoſe to our aſtoniſhed view "that undiſcovered country, from whoſe bourne no traveller returns."

SHAKESPEAR,

SHAKESPEAR, with whoſe words we concluded the laſt ſentence, is the only *Engliſh* writer, who with amazing boldneſs has ventured to burſt the barriers of a ſeparate ſtate, and diſcloſe the land of Apparitions, Shadows, and Dreams; and he has nobly ſucceeded in his daring attempt. His very peculiar excellence in this reſpect will be more properly illuſtrated in another part of our Eſſay. In the mean time we may obſerve, that it will be hazardous for any one to purſue the track which he has marked out; and that none but a Genius uncommonly original, can hope for ſucceſs in the purſuit.

Should ſuch a Genius ariſe, he could not deſire a nobler field for the diſplay of an exuberant Imagination, than what the ſpiritual world, with its ſtrange inhabitants, will preſent to him. In deſcribing the nature and employment of thoſe viſionary beings, whoſe exiſtence is fixed in a future ſtate, or of thoſe who exiſt in the preſent, or may be ſuppoſed to inhabit the "midway air," but

but are possessed of certain powers and faculties, very different from what are possessed by mankind, he is not, as in describing human characters, restricted to exact probability, much less to truth: for we are in most instances utterly ignorant of the powers of different or superior beings; and, consequently, are very incompetent judges of the probability or improbability of the particular influence, or actions attributed to them. All that we require of a Poet therefore, who pretends to exhibit characters of this kind, is, that the incidents, in effectuating which they are supposed to be concerned, be possible, and consonant to the general analogy of their nature; an analogy, founded not upon truth or strict probability, but upon common tradition or popular opinion. It is evident therefore that the Poet who would give us a glimpse of the other world, and an idea of the nature, employment, and manner of existence of those who inhabit it, or of those other imaginary beings, who are in some respects similar to, but in others totally

totally different from mankind, and are ſuppoſed to dwell on or about this earth, has abundant ſcope for the exerciſe of the moſt fertile Invention. This ideal region is indeed the proper ſphere of Fancy, in which ſhe may range with a looſe rein, without ſuffering reſtraint from the ſevere checks of Judgment; for Judgment has very little juriſdiction in this province of Fable. The invention of the ſupernatural characters above-mentioned, and the exhibition of them, with their proper attributes and offices, are the higheſt efforts and the moſt pregnant proofs of truly ORIGINAL GENIUS.

The third ſpecies of Invention, by which we obſerved original Genius will be diſtinguiſhed, is that of IMAGERY. The ſtile of an original Author in Poetry is for the moſt part FIGURATIVE and METAPHORICAL. The ordinary modes of ſpeech being unable to expreſs the grandeur or the ſtrength of his conceptions, appear FLAT and LANGUID to his ardent Imagination. In order therefore

to

to ſupply the poverty of common language, he has recourſe to METAPHORS and IMAGES *; which,

---

* LONGINUS is of opinion, that the uſe of metaphors and figures has an admirable effect in compoſition, both by heightening the ſublime, and giving greater force to the pathetic; and likewiſe obſerves, that while figures give a particular efficacy to the ſublime, they receive equal benefit from it in turn:

Εςαι δε πανυ συντομον, οτι φυσει πως συμμαχει τω υψει τα σχηματα, και παλιν αντισυμμαχειται θαυμαςως υπ' αυτε. *De Sublim.* ſect. 17.

He obſerves in another place, that the crowding figures together, is a method of exciting the more violent commotions of the mind:

Ακρως δε και η επι ταυτο συνοδος των σχηματων ειωθε κινειν, οταν δυο η τρια, οιον κατα συμμοριαν ανακιρναμενα, αλληλοις εραvιζε την ισχυν την πειθω το καλλος. *De Sublim.* ſect. 20.

QUINTILIAN admits of metaphors in an oration only, in order to fill up a vacant place, or when they have greater force than thoſe unornamented expreſſions in whoſe place they are ſubſtituted: "Metaphora enim "aut vacantem occupare locum debet, aut ſi in alie- "num venit, plus valere eo quod expellit." *Inſtit.* lib. viii. cap. 6. — If however we reflect, that Poetry, whoſe capital end it is to pleaſe, requires more ornament than Proſe compoſition, in order to the attainment

which, though they may ſometimes occaſion the want of preciſion, will always elevate his ſtile, as well as give a peculiar dignity and energy to his ſentiments *. An original Author indeed will frequently be apt to exceed in the uſe of this ornament, by pouring forth ſuch a blaze of imagery, as to dazzle and overpower the mental ſight; the effect of which is, that his Writings become obſcure †, if not unintelligible to common Readers;

ment of that end, we ſhall ſee the neceſſity of allowing to Poets greater licence in the uſe of metaphors and imagery, than to any other Authors whatever.

* "Sed illud quoque, de quo in argumentis diximus, ſimilitudinis genus ornat orationem, facitque ſublimem, floridam, jucundam, mirabilem." *Inſtit.* lib. viii. cap. 3. — The above remark, the Reader will obſerve, is ſtill more eminently true with reſpect to the influence of Imagery in Poetry.

† It is a maxim laid down by QUINTILIAN, that in an oration the image ſhould be clearer than that which it is adduced to illuſtrate: "Debet enim quod illuſtrandæ alterius rei gratia aſſumitur, ipſum eſſe clarius eo quod illuminat." *Ibid.* He obſerves a little

Readers; juſt as the eye is for ſome time rendered incapable of diſtinguiſhing the objects that are preſented to it, after having ſtedfaſtly contemplated the Sun. Well choſen images, happily adapted to the purpoſe for which they are adduced, if not too frequently employed, produce a fine effect in Poetry. They impart a pleaſing gratification to the mind, ariſing from the diſcovery of the reſemblance betwixt the ſimilitude and the object to which it is compared; they remarkably enliven deſcription, at the ſame time that they embelliſh it with additional graces *; they give force as well as

---

little above, that one of the eſſential excellencies of Imagery conſiſts in its being uſeful for illuſtration: "Præclare vero ad inferendam rebus lucem, repertæ "ſunt ſimilitudines." This likewiſe is one of its uſes in Poetry.

* QUINTILIAN, ſpeaking of metaphors, makes the following obſervation concerning them: "Tum "ita jucunda atque nitida, ut in oratione quamlibet "clara, proprio tamen lumine eluceat. Neque enim "vulgaris eſſe, nec humilis, nec inſuavis, recte modo "adſcita poteſt." *Inſtit.* lib. viii. cap. 6.

grandeur

grandeur to the ſtile of Poetry, and are a principal ſource of thoſe exquiſite ſenſations, which it is calculated to inſpire. On the other hand, the too liberal uſe of IMAGERY even in Poetry (beſides that obſcurity which it occaſions to the ordinary claſs of Readers, as well as that fatigue which the Imagination experiences from its exceſſive glare) ſo diſguſts the mind with the perpetual labour of tracing relations and reſemblances, which cannot always be immediately perceived, that the tide of paſſion is by this means diverted, if it doth not ſubſide, and the pleaſure ariſing from poetic imitation is greatly diminiſhed, if not utterly deſtroyed. A Writer however, who is only poſſeſſed of a moderate degree of Genius, is in very little hazard of falling into this extreme. His imagination is not extenſive enough to comprehend thoſe remote analogies which ſubſiſt betwixt different objects in nature, nor does it poſſeſs force ſufficient to throw off a bold and glowing image founded upon ſuch analogies: the performances of ſuch an Author therefore will either be intirely deſtitute of the images of Poetry, excepting ſuch as ariſe from the moſt obvious relations of ideas; or elſe thoſe which he adopts will be borrowed from Authors of ſuperior Genius. Hence it is, that the images of HOMER have been ſo often copied by modern Poets, who either poſſeſſed not fertility of Invention enough to ſtrike out new ſimilitudes for themſelves, or dared not to exert it. A Poet endued with a truly original Genius, will however be under no neceſſity of drawing any of the materials of his compoſition from the Works of preceding Bards; ſince he has an unfailing reſource in the exuberance of his own Imagination, which will furniſh him with a redundance of all thoſe materials, and particularly with an inexhauſtible variety of new and ſplendid imagery, which muſt be regarded as one diſtinguiſhing mark of original poetic Genius.

The fourth and laſt ſpecies of Invention, by which we obſerved this quality to be indicated,

dicated, was that of SENTIMENT. An original Genius in Poetry will ſtrike out NEW SENTIMENTS, as well as NEW IMAGES, on every ſubject on which he employs his talents; and he has the peculiar felicity of ſtriking out ſuch as are moſt proper to the ſubject and to the occaſion. An univerſal Genius is a very extraordinary phenomenon. Even a talent for acquiring excellence in the various branches of any one art, is very rarely beſtowed; ſo limited in general are the faculties of the human mind. Thus we ſeldom find a Genius for Tragedy and Comedy, or a Genius for the more ſublime ſpecies of Hiſtory-painting, and for pieces of Drollery and Humour in low life, united in the ſame perſon. We have already obſerved, in a note at the beginning of this ſection, that there are different kinds, as well as degrees of Originality; we are not therefore to expect, that an original Genius in Poetry ſhould attain eminence in every branch of his profeſſion; it is enough if he diſtinguiſh himſelf in one branch, whatever it may be. What we would be underſtood to maintain is this; that original Genius will dictate the moſt proper ſentiments on every ſubject, and in every ſpecies of Poetry, INDISCRIMINATELY; but that it will dictate the ſentiments moſt proper to that particular ſpecies to which it is ADAPTED, and to which it applies its inventive powers. If, for inſtance, we ſuppoſe this quality adapted to Epic Poetry, it will diſcover itſelf in the invention both of ſublime and pathetic ſentiments, which will at once excite aſtoniſhment, and penetrate the heart. To a perſon who poſſeſſes a talent for this higheſt ſpecies of Poetry, ſuch ſentiments are as it were congenial; they ariſe naturally and ſpontaneouſly to his imagination. The ſublime, in particular, is the proper walk of a great Genius, in which it delights to range, and in which alone it can diſplay its powers to advantage, or put forth its ſtrength. As ſuch a Genius always attempts to graſp the moſt ſtupendous objects,

jects *, it is much more delighted with surveying the rude magnificence of nature, than the elegant decorations of art; since the latter produce only an agreeable sensation of pleasure; but the former throws the soul into a divine transport of admiration † and amazement,

---

* Longinus, that admirable Critic, illustrates this observation very beautifully:

Ενθεν φυσικως πως αγομενοι μα δι ου τα μικρα ρειθρα θαυμαζομεν, ει και διαυγη και χρησιμα· αλλα τον Νειλον, και Ιστρον η Ρηνον, πολυ δ' ετι μαλλον τον Ωκεανον. Ου δε γε το υφ' ἡμων τουτι φλογιον ανακαιομενον, επει καθαρον σωζει το φεγγος, εκπληττομεθα των ουρανιων μαλλον, και τοι πολλακις επισκοτουμενων· ου δε των της Αιτνης κρατηρων αξιοθαυμαστοτερον νομιζομεν, ης αι αναχοαι πετρους τε εκ βυθου και ὁλους οχθους αναφερουσι, και ποταμους ενιοτε του γενους εκεινου και αυτου μονου προχεουσι πυρος. *De Sublim.* cap. 35.

† The above-mentioned excellent Author gives the following just description of the nature, characteristics, and effects of true sublimity:

Τουτο γαρ τω οντι μεγα, ου πολλη μεν ἡ αναθεωρησις, δυσκολος δε, μαλλον δ' αδυνατος ἡ κατεξαναστασις· ισχυρα δε ἡ μνημη, και δυσεξαλειπτος. Ὁλως δε καλα νομιζε ὑψη και αληθινα, τα δια παντος αρεσκοντα και πασιν. *Ibid.* cap. 7.

 The

amazement, which occupies and fills the mind, and at the ſame time inſpires that ſolemn dread, that religious awe, which naturally reſults from the contemplation of the vaſt and wonderful. By dwelling on ſuch ſubjects, the ſoul is elevated to a ſenſe of its own dignity and greatneſs.

We obſerved likewiſe, that an Author poſſeſſed of that kind and degree of original Genius which is adapted to Epic Poetry, will admirably ſucceed in the invention of

---

The *Roman* Critic judiciouſly obſerves, that in forming our opinion of ſublimity in compoſition, we ought to conſider the nature of the ſubject on which it is employed, and how far it is ſuitable to the kind of ornament made uſe of; becauſe, where the ſubject itſelf is mean, ſublimity degenerates into bombaſt:

" Clara illa atque ſublimia, plerunque materiæ modo
" cernenda ſunt. Quod enim alibi magnificum, tumi-
" dum alibi. Et quæ humilia circa res magnas, apta
" circa minores videntur. Et ſicut in oratione nitida
" notabile eſt humilius verbum, & velut macula: ita
" a ſermone tenui ſublime nitidumque diſcordat, fitque
" corruptum, quia in plano tumet." QUINT. *Inſtit.* lib. viii. cap. 3.

PATHETIC

PATHETIC * as well as SUBLIME ſentiments; if an Author can be ſaid to invent ſentiments which riſe to the imagination, in a manner by a ſimple volition, without any labour, and almoſt without any effort. Such a perſon being endued with a vivacity and vigour of Imagination, as well as an exquiſite ſenſibility of every emotion, whether pleaſant or painful, which can affect the human heart, has nothing elſe to do, in order to move the paſſions of others, but to repreſent his own feelings in a ſtrong and lively manner; and to exhibit the object, event or action he propoſes to deſcribe, in that particular attitude or view, which has moſt powerfully intereſted his own affec-

* This talent of raiſing the paſſions by ſuitable repreſentations, ſeems to depend upon an extreme ſenſibility both of pain and pleaſure, joined to the power of deſcribing in a lively manner thoſe exquiſite ſenſations which we ourſelves feel. Both the one and the other are the inſeparable concomitants of true Genius; tho' there are many poſſeſſed of the former, who are not endued with the latter.

tions,

tions, for that will moſt certainly intereſt ours: we ſhall feel the ſame concern, and ſhare in the ſame diſtreſs *. Having by this means gained an aſcendant over our hearts, he will at pleaſure melt them into tenderneſs and pity, or fire them with indignation and rage: every paſſion will be obedient to his impulſe, as well as ſubject to his controul; like the Poet deſcribed by HORACE, he will raiſe in our ſouls

---

*. ARISTOTLE obſerves, in his book on Poetry, that there are various methods of raiſing the paſſions; that pity and terror may be excited by external action, particularly by the ſymptoms of diſtreſs ſtrongly impreſſed upon the countenance; but that a good Poet will never have recourſe to this method as his only expedient for moving the paſſions, but will accompliſh his end by the very conſtitution of his fable, and the affecting nature of the relation itſelf:

Εστι μεν ουν το φοβερον και ελεεινον εκ της οψεως γινεσθαι. Εστι δε και εξ αυτης της συστασεως των πραγματων, όπερ εστι προτερον και ποιητου αμεινονος. Δει γαρ και ανευ του όραν ούτω συνεστακαι τον μυθον ώστε τον ακουοντα τα πραγματα γινομενα, και φριττειν και ελεειν εκ των συμβαινοντων. cap. 14.

every

every emotion of which they are susceptible †:

Irritat, mulcet, falsis terroribus implet
Ut magus, et modo me Thebis, modo ponit Athenis.

'Tis he who gives my breast a thousand pains,
Can make me feel each passion that he feigns;
Enrage, compose with more than magic art;
With pity and with terror tear my heart;
And snatch me o'er the earth, or thro' the air,
To *Thebes*, to *Athens*, when he will, and where.

POPE.

The

† QUINTILIAN considers the raising the passions of the hearers, and carrying them along by the force of rapid eloquence, as the highest effort of rhetorical Genius; and observes, that though many of his predecessors and cotemporaries in the rhetorical art excelled in the argumentative part of eloquence, few had excelled in the pathetic:

"Qui vero judicem rapere, & in quem vellet habi-
"tum animi posset perducere, quo dicto flendum &
"irascendum esset rarius fuit. Atque hoc est quod
"dominatur in judiciis; hæc eloquentiam regunt."
Lib. vi. *cap.* 3.

With

The ſentiments of an Author of this kind * are the natural dictates of the heart, not fictitious or copied, but original; and it is impoſſible they ſhould fail in producing their proper effect upon the mind of the Reader. Theſe obſervations, by which we have endeavoured to ſhew how originality of Genius in the higher ſpecies of Poetry will diſcover itſelf in the invention of ſen-

---

With reſpect to the higher ſpecies of Poetry, Tragedy and the *Epopœa*, it is needleſs to ſay how much the pathetic ought to predominate in them; and that to the attainment of it in an extraordinary degree, an eminent exertion of poetic Genius is eſſentially requiſite.

* In order to intereſt our affections deeply in any cauſe, and raiſe our paſſions to the higheſt degree, LONGINUS requires that the emotion and agitation of the Orator who addreſſes us, ſhould appear not to be mechanical or premeditated, but to riſe immediately from the ſubject and the occaſion; in which caſe he obſerves, we ſhall always feel our minds moſt powerfully affected:

Αγει γαρ τα παθητικα τοτε μαλλον, οταν αυτα φαινηται μη επιτηδευειν αυτος ὁ λεγων, αλλα γεννᾷν ὁ καιρος. *De Sublim.* cap. 18.

timent,

timent, are equally applicable to its inferior ſpecies; ſince, as we have obſerved, original Genius will diſtinguiſh itſelf by the invention of NEW ſentiments on every ſubject to which it applies itſelf.

Having conſidered the different ſpecies of INVENTION, which appear to be characteriſtical of original Genius, we ſhall point out ſome other properties which indicate and diſtinguiſh it.

Vivid and picturеſque deſcription, therefore, we conſider as one of theſe. In the ſphere of Poetry, there is an infinite variety of objects and ſcenes, adapted to the different taſtes of thoſe who contemplate them. A Writer however, of the kind above-mentioned, diſregarding the beauties of a common landſcape, fixes his eye on thoſe delightful and unfrequented retreats, which are impervious to common view: to drop the metaphor, out of the multiplicity of ſubjects which his imagination preſents to him, he he ſelects ſuch as are moſt ſuſceptible of the graces of poetic deſcription, and adorns theſe with all the luxuriance of an exuberant Imagination. We ſhall readily confeſs, that a talent for deſcription is by no means ſo RADICAL and DISTINGUISHING a quality in the conſtitution of original Genius, as any of the ſpecies of INVENTION above-mentioned; yet this talent, when poſſeſſed in a high degree, bears alſo the ſtamp of originality, however the impreſſion may be ſomewhat fainter; and in the deſcriptive pieces of an original Author, we can trace the vivacity, the wildneſs, and the ſtrength of his Imagination. Such pieces will always be eaſily diſtinguiſhed from thoſe of an inferior Author, which, in compariſon with the former, will be languid, trivial, and common.

A perſon who is deſtitute of Genius, diſcovers nothing new or diſcriminating in the objects which he ſurveys. He takes only a general and ſuperficial view of them, and is incapable of discerning those minute properties, or of relishing those particular and distinguishing beauties, which a lively Imagination, united with an exquisite Taste, can alone enable a man to conceive and admire. The descriptions of such a person (if he attempts to describe) must necessarily be unanimated, undistinguishing, and uninteresting; for as his imagination hath presented to him no distinct or vivid idea of the scenes or objects he has contemplated, it is impossible he should be able to give a particular and picturesque representation of it to others. A Poet, on the other hand, who is possessed of original Genius, feels in the strongest manner every impression made upon the mind, by the influence of external objects on the senses, or by reflection on those ideas which are treasured up in the repository of the memory, and is consequently qualified to express the vivacity and strength of his own feelings. If we suppose a person endued with this quality to describe real objects and scenes, such as are either immedi-

ately

ately preſent to his ſenſes, or recent in his remembrance; he will paint them in ſuch vivid colours, and with ſo many picturesque circumſtances, as to convey the ſame lively and fervid ideas to the mind of the Reader, which poſſeſſed and filled the imagination of the Author. If we ſuppoſe him to deſcribe unreal objects or ſcenes, ſuch as exiſt not in nature, but may be ſuppoſed to exiſt, he will preſent to us a ſucceſſion of theſe equally various and wonderful, the mere creation of his own fancy; and by the ſtrength of his repreſentation, will give to an illuſion all the force and efficacy of a reality. As all his deſcriptions will be vivid, ſo all his ſcenery will be rich and luxuriant in the higheſt degree, ſo as to evidence the extent, the copiouſneſs, and the fertility of his imagination.

That vivacity of deſcription, which we have obſerved to be characteriſtical of a great Genius, will in the writings of an original one be of a kind peculiar and uncommon.

mon. Objects or events may be viewed in very different lights by different perſons, and admit of great variety in the repreſentation. In the deſcriptions wherein ſublimity is required, an Author of original Genius will fix on thoſe circumſtances that may raiſe our ideas of the object he endeavours to repreſent to the utmoſt pitch. Thus the enraptured Prophet, in deſcribing the deſcent of the Almighty, is not contented with repreſenting the inhabitants of the earth as in a conſternation, and the whole maſs of matter as agitated at his approach; but riſes much higher in his deſcription, and gives ſenſe as well as motion to the inanimate parts of the creation: *The mountains ſaw thee, and they trembled; the overflowing of the water paſſed by.* Then follows a bold and happy proſopopœia: *The Deep uttered his voice, and lift up his hands on high.* The former part of the deſcription, where the Prophet makes the mountains ſenſible of the approach, and tremble at the preſence of JEHOVAH, is truly ſublime, as theſe effects give us a high idea of the majeſty and power of the Almighty; but the latter part of it, where he attributes voice and action to the great Deep, is remarkably grand, and is indeed one of the moſt ſtriking and daring perſonifications that are to be met with either in the ſacred or profane writings. It is by fixing on ſuch great and uncommon circumſtances, that an original Author diſcovers the ſublimity of his Genius; circumſtances which, at the ſame time that they ſhew the immenſity of his conceptions, raiſe our admiration and aſtoniſhment to the higheſt degree.

To the particular and eſſential ingredients of original Genius above enumerated, we ſhall ſubjoin three others of a more general nature; which however are as characteriſtical of this uncommon endowment, and as much diſtinguiſh its productions, as any of the particular properties above ſpecified. Theſe are an IRREGULAR GREATNESS, WILDNESS, and ENTHUSIASM of Imagination. The qualities we have juſt now mentioned

mentioned are diſtinct from each other; but as they are nearly allied, and are commonly found together, we include them in one claſs, conſidering them as unitedly forming one general indication of elevated and original Genius; though, for the ſake of preciſion, we ſhall treat of them ſeparately.

Firſt we obſerved, that IRREGULAR GREATNESS of Imagination was characteriſtical of ORIGINAL GENIUS. This expreſſion is a little equivocal in its ſignification, and therefore it will be neceſſary to aſcertain the ſenſe in which we conſider it.

An IRREGULAR GREATNESS of Imagination is ſometimes ſuppoſed to imply a mixture of great beauties and blemiſhes, blended together in any work of Genius; and thus we frequently apply it to the writings of SHAKESPEAR, whoſe excellencies are as tranſcendent, as his faults are conſpicuous. Without rejecting this ſenſe altogether, or denying that an original Author will be diſtinguiſhed by his imperfections as well as by his excellencies, we may obſerve, that the expreſſion above-mentioned is capable of a juſter and more determinate meaning than that juſt ſpecified. It may, we think, be more properly underſtood to ſignify that native grandeur of ſentiment which diſclaims all reſtraint, is ſubject to no certain rule, and is therefore various and unequal. In this ſenſe principally we conſider the expreſſion, and are under no difficulty in declaring, that an irregular greatneſs of Imagination, as thus explained, is one remarkable criterion of exalted and original Genius. A perſon who is poſſeſſed of this quality, naturally turns his thoughts to the contemplation of the Grand and Wonderful, in nature or in human life, in the viſible creation, or in that of his own fancy. Revolving theſe awful and magnificent ſcenes in his muſing mind, he labours to expreſs in his compoſitions the ideas

which

which dilate and ſwell his Imagination; but is often unſucceſsful in his efforts. In attempting to repreſent theſe, he feels himſelf embarraſſed; words are too weak to convey the ardor of his ſentiments, and he frequently ſinks under the immenſity of his own conceptions. Sometimes indeed he will be happy enough to paint his very thought, and to excite in others the very ſentiments which he himſelf feels: he will not always however ſucceed ſo well, but, on the contrary, will often labour in a fruitleſs attempt; whence it ſhould ſeem, that his compoſition will upon certain occaſions be diſtinguiſhed by an irregular and unequal greatneſs.

Whether this quality is to be aſcribed to the cauſe above-mentioned in particular; or whether it is the effect of that fiery impetuoſity of Imagination, which, breaking through the legal reſtraints of criticiſm, or overleaping the mounds of authority and cuſtom, ſometimes loſes ſight of the Juſt and Natural, while it is in purſuit of the New and Wonderful, and, by attempting to riſe above the ſphere of Humanity, tumbles from its towering height; or laſtly, whether it is to be ultimately derived from the unavoidable imperfection of the human faculties, which admit not of perpetual extenſion, and are apt to flag in a long, though rapid flight; whichſoever of theſe may be the cauſe of the phenomenon above-mentioned, or whether all of them may contribute to produce it, certain it is, that an irregular greatneſs of Imagination, implying unequal and diſproportioned grandeur, is always diſcernible in the compoſitions of an original Genius, however elevated, and is therefore an univerſal characteriſtic of ſuch a Genius *.

It

* LONGINUS maintains, that a high degree of ſublimity is utterly inconſiſtent with accuracy of imagination; and that Authors of the moſt elevated Genius, at the ſame time that they are capable of riſing to the greateſt excellencies, are likewiſe moſt apt to commit trivial

It deſerves however to be obſerved, that the imperfection here ſuggeſted, is a natural effect and a certain proof of an exuberant Imagination. Ordinary minds ſeldom riſe above the dull uniform tenor of common ſentiments, like thoſe animals that are condemned to creep on the ground all the days of their life; but the moſt lawleſs excurſions of an original Genius, like the flight of an eagle, are towering, though devious; its path, as the courſe of a comet, is blazing, though irregular; and its

---

trivial faults, while they are aiming at diſtinguiſhed beauties. As this aſſertion is pretty nearly of the ſame import with that above advanced, it may not be improper to confirm our ſentiments by the authority of ſo eminent a Critic:

Εγω δ' οιδα μεν, ὡς αἱ ὑπερβολαι μεγεθες φυσει ἡκιςα καθαραι. Το γαρ εν παντι ακριβες, κινδυνος σμικροτητος· εν δε τοις μεγεθεσιν, ωσπερ εν τοις αγαν πλουτοις, ειναι τι χρη και παρολιγωρουμενον. Μη ποτε δε τουτο και αναγκαιον η, το τας μεν ταπεινας και μεσας φυσεις, δια το μηδαμη παρακινδυνευειν, μηδε εφιεσθαι των ακρων, αναμαρτητους ως επι το πολυ και ασφαλεςερας διαμενειν· τα δε μεγαλα επισφαλη δι αυτο γινεσθαι το μεγεθος. *De Sublim.* ſect. 33.

errors and excellencies are equally inimitable.

We obſerved that original Genius is likewiſe diſtinguiſhed by a WILDNESS of Imagination. This quality, ſo cloſely allied to the former, ſeems alſo to proceed from the ſame cauſes; and is at the ſame time an infallible proof of a fertile and luxuriant fancy. WILDNESS of imagery, ſcenery and ſentiment, is the PASTIME of a playful and ſportive Imagination; it is the effect of its exuberance. This character is formed by an arbitrary aſſemblage of the moſt extravagant, uncommon, and romantic ideas, united in the moſt fanciful combinations; and is diſplayed in groteſque figures, in ſurpriſing ſentiments, in pictureſque and inchanting deſcription. The quality of which we are treating, wherever it is diſcovered, will afford ſuch a delicious entertainment to the mind, that it can ſcarce be ever ſatisfied with a banquet ſo exquiſitely prepared; ſatiety being prevented by a ſuca ſucceſſion of dainties, ever various and ever new.

The laſt quality by which we affirmed original Genius to be characteriſed, was an ENTHUSIASM of Imagination *. It frequently

quently

* Thoſe who have a curioſity to know the opinion of PLATO concerning the ENTHUSIASM of Poetry, may conſult his *Io*; where he expreſly aſſerts, that all true Poets are divinely inſpired by the Muſes; that they are incapable in their ſober ſenſes to compoſe good verſes; and that therefore, in order to their becoming excellent in their profeſſion, it is neceſſary they ſhould be hurried out of themſelves, and, like Bacchanals, be tranſported by a kind of divine fury. As his opinion, however, upon this point, will give a ſtrong ſanction to our ſentiments on that Enthuſiaſm of Imagination which we have obſerved to diſtinguiſh original poetic Genius, we ſhall preſent the Reader with two ſhort extracts from the above-mentioned Dialogue, very expreſſive of his idea concerning poetic Inſpiration:

Ουτω δε και η Μουσα ενθεους μεν ποιει αυτη, δια δε των ενθεων τουτων αλλων ενθουσιαζοντων, ορμαθος εξαρταται. *Io.* p. 364.

SOCRATES (for he is the ſpeaker) adds a little after

Λεγουσι μεν δηπουθεν προς ἡμας οἱ ποιηται ὁτι απο κρηνων μελιρρυτων, εκ Μουσων κηπων τινων και ναπων δρεπομενοι τα μελη

ἡμιν

quently happens, that the original meaning of a word is loſt or become obſolete, and another very different one, through accident, cuſtom or caprice, is ordinarily ſubſtituted in its place. Sometimes expreſſions, which have been anciently taken in a good ſenſe, are, by a ſtrange perverſion of language, uſed in a bad one; and by this means they become obnoxious upon account of the ideas, which, in their common acceptation they excite. This is the caſe with the word ENTHUSIASM, which is almoſt univerſally taken in a bad ſenſe; and, being conceived to proceed from an overheated and diſtempered imagination, is ſuppoſed to imply weakneſs, ſuperſtition, and madneſs. ENTHUSIASM, in this modern ſenſe, is in no reſpect a qualification of a Poet;

ημιν φερουσιν ὡσπερ ἁι μελιτται, και αυτοι ὁυτω πετρομενοι. Και αληθη λεγουσι· κουφον γαρ χρημα ποιητης εστι, και πτηνον, και ιερον. Και ου πρωτερον οιος τε ποιειν πριν αν ενθεος τε γενηται και εκφρων, και ὁ νους μηκετι εν αυτω ενη· ἑως δ' αν τουτι εχη το κτημα, αδυνατος παν ποιειν εστιν ανθρωπος, η χρησμῳδειν. *Ibid.*

in the ancient ſenſe, which implied a kind of divine INSPIRATION †, or an ardor of Fancy wrought up to Tranſport, we not only admit, but deem it an eſſential one.

A glowing ardor of Imagination is indeed (if we may be permitted the expreſſion) the very ſoul of Poetry. It is the principal ſource of INSPIRATION; and the Poet who is poſſeſſed of it, like the *Delphian* Prieſteſs, is animated with a kind of DIVINE FURY. The intenſeneſs and vigour of his ſenſations produce that ENTHUSIASM of Imagination, which as it were hurries the mind out of itſelf; and which is vented in warm and vehement deſcription, exciting in every ſuſceptible breaſt the ſame emotions that were felt by the Author himſelf. It is this ENTHUSIASM which gives life and ſtrength to poetical repreſentations, renders them ſtriking imitations of nature, and thereby

† The etymology of the word ENTHUSIASM, which is ενθεος, will aſcertain its original ſenſe.

produces

produces that inchanting delight which genuine Poetry is calculated to inſpire. Without this animating principle, all poetical and rhetorical compoſitions are ſpiritleſs and languid, like thoſe bodies that are drained of their vital juices: they are therefore read with indifference or inſipidity; the harmony of the numbers, if harmonious, may tickle the ear, but being deſtitute of nerves, that is of paſſion and ſentiment, they can never affect the heart.

Thus we have pointed out and illuſtrated the moſt diſtinguiſhing ingredients of ORIGINAL GENIUS in Poetry; we ſhall conclude the preſent ſection with inquiring into the firſt and moſt natural exertions of Genius in this divine art.

We may venture then to lay it down as a poſition highly probable, that the firſt eſſays of original Genius will be in ALLEGORIES, VISIONS, or the creation of ideal beings, of one kind or another. There is

no

no kind of Invention, in which there is fuller ſcope afforded to the exerciſe of Imagination, than in that of ALLEGORY; which has this advantage over moſt other fables, that in it the Author is by no means reſtricted to ſuch an exact probability, as is required in thoſe fables that inſtruct us by a repreſentation of actions, which, though not real, muſt always however be ſuch as might have happened. Let it be obſerved, that we are here ſpeaking of ALLEGORY in its utmoſt latitude. We are not ignorant that there is a ſpecies of it, which, like the Epic fable, attempts to inſtruct by the invention of a ſeries of incidents ſtrictly probable. Such are the beautiful and ſtriking ALLEGORIES contained in different parts of the Sacred Writings. But there is another kind of ALLEGORICAL fable, in which there is very little regard ſhewn to probability. Its object alſo is inſtruction; though it does not endeavour to inſtruct by real or probable actions; but wrapt in a veil of exaggerated, yet delicate and appoſite fic-

tion,

tion, is ſtudious at once to delight the imagination, and to impreſs ſome important maxim upon the mind. Of this kind is the *Fairy Queen* of SPENSER. As in this ſpecies of ALLEGORY, we neither expect what is true, nor what is like the truth; ſo we read ſuch fabulous compoſitions, partly for the ſake of the morals they contain, but principally for the ſake of gratifying that curioſity ſo deeply implanted in the human mind, of becoming acquainted with new and marvellous events. We are in this caſe in a great meaſure upon our guard againſt the deluſions of fancy; are highly pleaſed with the narrative, though we do not allow it to impoſe upon us ſo far as to obtain our credit. Yet ſuch is the power of ingenious fiction over our minds, that we are not only captivated and intereſted by a relation of ſurpriſing incidents, though very improbable, but, during the time of the relation at leaſt, we forget that they are fictitious, and almoſt fancy them to be real. This deceit, however,

however, lafts no longer than the perufal, in which we are too much agitated to reflect on the probability or improbability of the events related; but when that is over, the inchantment vanifhes in the cool moment of deliberation; and, being left at leifure to think and reafon, we never admit as true what is not ftrictly probable.

As we are treating of allegorical fables, it may not be amifs to obferve, with regard to the kind laft mentioned in particular, that the liberties indulged to it, though prodigioufly various and extenfive, are not however without certain reftrictions. Thus, though we do not require probability in the general contexture of the fable, juftnefs of manners muft be preferved in this, as well as in the other fpecies of fabulous compofition; the incidents muft be fuitable to the characters to which they are accommodated; thofe incidents muft likewife clearly point out or imply

imply the moral they are intended to illustrate; and they muſt, in order to captivate the Imagination, be new and ſurpriſing, at the ſame time that they are to be perfectly conſiſtent with each other. It is evident however, that theſe ſlight reſtraints prove no real impediment to the natural impulſe and excurſions of Genius, but that they ſerve rather to point and regulate its courſe. It is likewiſe equally evident, that this laſt mentioned ſpecies of Allegory preſents a noble field for the diſplay of a rich and luxuriant Imagination; and that to excel in it, requires the utmoſt fertility of Invention, ſince every maſterly compoſition of this kind muſt be the mere creation of the Poet's fancy.

We obſerved likewiſe, that ORIGINAL GENIUS will naturally diſcover itſelf in VISIONS. This is a ſpecies of fiction, to ſucceed in which with applauſe, requires as much poetic Inſpiration as any other ſpecies of compoſition whatever. That Enthu-

ſiaſm

ſiaſm of Imagination, which we conſidered as an eſſential characteriſtic of original Genius, is indiſpenſibly neceſſary to the enraptured Bard, who would make his Readers feel thoſe impetuous tranſports of paſſion which occupy and actuate his own mind. He muſt himſelf be wrought up to a high pitch of extaſy, if he expects to throw us into it. Indeed it is the peculiar felicity of an original Author to feel in the moſt exquiſite degree every emotion, and to ſee every ſcene he deſcribes. By the vigorous effort of a creative Imagination, he calls ſhadowy ſubſtances and unreal objects into exiſtence. They are preſent to his view, and glide, like ſpectres, in ſilent, ſullen majeſty, before his aſtoniſhed and intranced ſight. In reading the deſcription of ſuch apparitions, we partake of the Author's emotion; the blood runs chill in our veins, and our hair ſtiffens with horror.

It would far exceed the bounds preſcribed to this Eſſay, to point out all the particular tracks which an original Genius will ſtrike out in the extenſive ſphere of Imagination, as thoſe paths are ſo various and devious. In the mean time we may obſerve, that as the hand of Nature hath ſtamped different minds with a different kind and degree of Originality, giving each a particular bent to one certain object or purſuit; original Authors will purſue the track marked out by Nature, by faithfully following which they can alone hope for immortality to their writings and reputation. Thus while one Writer, obeying the impulſe of his Genius, diſplays the exuberance of his Fancy in the beautiful and ſurpriſing fictions of Allegory; another diſcovers the fertility and extent of his Imagination as well as the juſtneſs of his Judgment, in the conduct of the Epic or Dramatic Fable, in which he raiſes our admiration, our terror, or our pity, as occaſion may require.

Upon the whole, we need not heſitate to affirm, that original Genius will probably diſcover

diſcover itſelf either in ALLEGORIES, VISIONS, or in the creation of ideal figures of one kind or another. The probability that it will do ſo, is derived from that innate tendency to FICTION which diſtinguiſhes ſuch a Genius, and from the natural bias of FICTION to run in this particular channel: for the Imagination of a Poet, whoſe Genius is truly Original, finding no objects in the viſible creation ſufficiently marvellous and new, or which can give full ſcope to the exerciſe of its powers, naturally burſts into the ideal world, in queſt of more ſurpriſing and wonderful ſcenes, which it explores with inſatiable curioſity, as well as with exquiſite pleaſure; and depending in its excurſion wholly on its own ſtrength, its ſucceſs in this province of FICTION will be proportionable to the plaſtic power of which it is poſſeſſed. In caſe however the poſition juſt advanced ſhould appear problematical to ſome, we ſhall confirm it by arguments drawn from experience, which will ſerve to ſhew, that ORIGINAL POETIC

GENIUS hath in fact exerted its powers in the manner above ſpecified *.

In proof of this aſſertion, we might adduce the whole ſyſtem of heathen Mytho-

---

* LONGINUS conſiders the introducing viſions into compoſition, and the ſupporting them with propriety, as one of the boldeſt efforts either of Rhetorical or Poetic Genius. He obſerves, that they contribute much to the grandeur, to the ſplendor, and to the efficacy of an oration in particular:

Ογκȣ και μεγαληγοριας, και αγωνος επι τȣτοις, ω νεανια, και αἱ φαντασιαι παρασκευαστικωταται· ειδωλοποιΐας αυτας ενιοι λεγουσι. Καλειται μεν γαρ κοινως φαντασια, παν εννοημα λογου γεννητικον οπωσȣν παριστaμενον· ιδιως δ' επι τȣτων κεκρατηκε τȣνομα, όταν ἁ λεγης, ὑπ' ενθȣσιασμȣ και παθȣς βλεπειν δοκης, και ὑπ' οψιν τιθης τοις ακȣουσιν. *De Sublim.* ſect. 15.

After having given this account of the nature and effect of a viſion introduced into an oration, he obſerves, that there is a difference betwixt viſions adapted to Rhetoric, and ſuch as are adapted to Poetry; but that they both concur in producing a violent commotion of mind:

Ως δ' ἑτερον τι ἡ ῥητορικη φαντασια βȣλεται, καὶ ἑτερον ἡ παρα ποιηταις, ȣκ αν λαθοι σε, ȣδ' ὁτι της μεν εν ποιησει τελος εστιν εκπληξις, της δ' εν λογοις εναργειά· ἀμφοτεραι δ' ὁμως τȣτ' επιζητουσι το συγκεκινημενον. *Ibid.*

logy.

logy. What are all the fabulous and allegorical relations of antiquity concerning the nature, generation, powers and offices of the Pagan Deities, but the inventions of men of Genius? Poets and Priests were unquestionably the original Authors of all the Theological Systems of the Gentile world. A ray, ultimately derived from divine Revelation, did sometimes indeed burst through the cloud of human error, but was soon obscured, if not smothered, by the superstitions of men; and oral Tradition, that fallacious guide, was buried under a mass of absurdity and folly. Though the heathen Theology must be confessed to be the disgrace and degradation of human reason, yet it must also be acknowledged to be a remarkable proof of the creative power of human Imagination; and at the same time that we condemn it as a religious Creed, we must admire it as a system of ingenious Fiction. The *Greek* Theology was of all other systems the most ingenious. What a strange, but fanciful account, may we collect from those ancient Authors, HOMER and HESIOD, of the nature and employment of the numerous Deities which *Greece* acknowledged? We find the celestial Divinities, JUPITER and JUNO, MINERVA and VENUS, MARS and APOLLO, sometimes quaffing nectar in their golden cups, and reposing themselves in indolent tranquillity, served by HEBE, and attended by MERCURY, the swift-winged messenger of the Gods: at other times we see them mixing among the *Trojan* and *Grecian* hosts, taking part in mortal quarrels, as partiality or favour dictated; inspiring the army whose cause they embraced with their counsel, and aiding it by their power; driving on or stemming the tide of battle, and alternately hastening and retarding the decrees of fate. CERES has the earth for her province, and is the bounteous giver of the golden grain; NEPTUNE sways the ocean with his trident; and PLUTO, seated on his throne in gloomy majesty, rules the dominions of the world below. Need we mention, as proofs of wild

and

and exuberant Fancy, the pleaſures and beauties of *Elyſium*, contraſted with the torments and horrors of dark *Tartarus*? Need we mention the black *Cocytus*, the flaming *Phlegethon*; the puniſhment of TANTALUS, the ever-rolling ſtone of SISYPHUS, the wheel of IXION, and the fruitleſs perpetual labours of the *Danaids*?

It would be impracticable, as well as tedious and unneceſſary to enumerate the vaſt multitude of ſubordinate Deities which *Greece* adored. All nature was repleniſhed with them; and each particular part had its tutelar Divinity. Thus while DIANA and her train of woodland nymphs, together with her miniſters the *Dryads* and *Hamadryads*, were adored by huntſmen as the Sovereigns of the woods, PAN received the homage of the ſimple ſhepherds, was conſidered as the Guardian of their flocks, and the rural God who taught them to play on the oaten pipe. To theſe we may join the Satyrs and Fawns, the *Naiads* of the rivers ſporting on the limpid ſtream, and the nymphs of the ſea riſing with THETIS from their watry beds, and lightly floating on the ſurface of the waves; the ſtory of PROMETHEUS chained to a rock, and devoured by vulturs, for ſtealing fire from Heaven, to animate his workmanſhip of clay; the loves of JUPITER and LEDA; the fable of MINERVA's iſſuing from the head of JUPITER; the wars of the latter with the Giants, and the fiction of VULCAN's being hurled from Heaven, with hideous ruin and combuſtion, by the wrath of the *Olympian* King. We may farther add thoſe exquiſite inventions of the Muſes and Graces, of Fortune and the Fates, of Auguries and Oracles, of the ſprings of *Helicon*, and inſpirations of *Parnaſſus*, the dreams of *Pindus* and the *Aonian* maids; the expedition of the *Argonauts*; the labours of HERCULES and of THESEUS; the fabulous, but pleaſing relations of the golden age; the contention of the Goddeſſes on mount *Ida*, for the prize of beauty; the admirable allegory of PRODICUS, in which Virtue

Virtue and Pleaſure are introduced as addreſſing HERCULES, and the excellent allegorical picture of human life by CEBES: all which ingenious fables conſidered together, and many more of them that might be mentioned, are ſtriking indications of the plaſtic power of the human mind, and undeniable proofs of true Genius in the original Inventers.

From this general and imperfect view of the *Greek* Mythology, it is evident, that original Genius did in ancient *Greece* always diſcover itſelf in allegorical Fiction, or in the creation of ideal figures of one kind or another; in inventing and adding new fables to the received ſyſtem of Mythology, or in altering and improving thoſe that had been already invented. The immenſe and multifarious ſyſtem of the *Greek* Theology was a work of many centuries, and roſe gradually to that height in which it now appears. Some additions were daily made to it by the Poets and men of lively Imagination,

nation, till that huge pile of Superſtition was completed, which, in its ruins, exhibits ſo ſtriking a monument of human ingenuity and folly. If, after what has been alledged, any one ſhould queſtion whether the fabulous Theology now conſidered, be an effect or indication of ORIGINAL GENIUS, we would only deſire him to ſuppoſe the Mythology of HOMER annihilated. What a blank would ſuch annihilation make in the divine *Iliad!* Deſtitute of its celeſtial machinery, would it not be in a great meaſure an inanimate maſs? It would at leaſt loſe much of that variety, dignity and grandeur, which we admire in it at preſent, and much of that pleaſing and ſurpriſing fiction, which gives ſuch exquiſite delight to the Imagination.

It would be eaſy to confirm the poſition we have laid down, that ORIGINAL GENIUS always diſcovers itſelf in Allegories, Viſions, or the invention of ideal Characters, by examples drawn from the Eaſtern and the

Egyptian

Egyptian Mythology, which was ſo full of Fable and hieroglyphical Emblems; but we ſhall wave the conſideration of theſe as ſuperfluous, after what hath been already urged, and conclude this part of our ſubject with obſerving, that the Eaſtern manner of writing is, and hath ever been characteriſed by a remarkable boldneſs of ſentiment and expreſſion, by the moſt rhetorical and poetical figures of ſpeech; and that many of the compoſitions of the Eaſtern nations abound with Allegories, Viſions and Dreams; of which we have ſeveral admirable examples in the ſacred Writings.

SECTION

SECTION IV.

OF ORIGINAL GENIUS IN THE OTHER FINE ARTS.

THOUGH it is Poetry that affords the amplest scope for the exertion of the powers of Imagination, and for the most advantageous display of ORIGINAL GENIUS; yet a very high degree of this quality may be discovered in some of the other fine Arts, and a greater or less degree of it in all of them; as they are all indebted, though not equally, to that faculty by which we have

have ſhewn true Genius to be principally conſtituted.

Having conſidered the exertions of ORIGINAL GENIUS in Poetry at great length in the preceding ſection, which indeed was the principal intention of this Eſſay we ſhall in the preſent ſection, in order to render the deſign more complete, point out, though with greater brevity, the efforts of GENIUS in the other liberal Arts, and endeavour to aſcertain the degree in which it will exert itſelf in each of them. Of theſe the art of Painting claims our firſt attention.

To an eminence in certain branches of this art, the greateſt ſhare of Imagination, next to what is required in Poetry, ſeems to be eſſentially neceſſary. Other branches however there are, in which a much leſs proportion of this talent is requiſite, and in which indeed ORIGINAL GENIUS cannot be diſplayed. We omit, as foreign to our purpoſe,

pose, the consideration of these inferior departments in the art of Painting, though successful attempts in them may indicate a great deal of ingenuity and skill; regarding only those higher classes, in which ORIGINAL GENIUS may exert itself to advantage.

We may observe in general, that as the power of INVENTION is the distinguishing ingredient of ORIGINAL GENIUS in all the fine Arts, as well as in Science; so, in whatever degree INVENTION is displayed in either of these, in the same degree ORIGINALITY of Genius will always be discovered. This distinction will exclude all PORTRAITS in Painting, however excellent, and many DESCRIPTIVE PIECES in Poetry, though copied from nature, from any pretensions to ORIGINALITY, strictly considered. Both may discover great vivacity and strength of Imagination; but as there is no fiction, nothing invented in either, they can only be regarded at best as the first and most

complete

complete COPIES of the true ORIGINALS. In common language indeed we talk of ORIGINAL portraits. by which we mean pictures drawn from the life. The propriety of this epithet we ſhall not diſpute. Such pictures are unqueſtionably in one ſenſe ORIGINAL, as they are the firſt draughts, of which the ſucceeding ones are but COPIES. In ſtrictneſs of ſpeech however, ſuch draughts themſelves are only the COPIES or RESEMBLANCES of Nature, to execute which does not require INVENTION, and conſequently does not indicate or preſuppoſe ORIGINALITY of Genius. We muſt therefore have recourſe to ſome higher branch of the art we are treating of, where this talent may be diſplayed to advantage, and that branch is HISTORY-PAINTING.

The Hiſtory Painter *, as well as the Epic

---

* As Poetry and Painting are in moſt reſpects ſimilar, it will be no incurious inquiry to examine into the

Epic Poet, commonly takes the ſubject of

---

the degree of Imagination requiſite to form an eminent Painter, compared with that which is neceſſary to form a great Poet. Every one who is in any meaſure acquainted with the reſpective natures of the above-mentioned arts, muſt obſerve a very cloſe affinity betwixt them, and that to excel in either of them a very high degree of Imagination is indiſpenſibly required. An accurate obſerver however will diſcover the different proportions of this quality that are appropriated and requiſite to each. Having one common end in view, the repreſentation of human characters, paſſions and events, or the repreſentation of thoſe objects which are either preſented to the ſenſes, or are the creation of fancy, he will perceive that they both accompliſh this end by IMITATION, though by a different kind of it. The Poet repreſents the objects of which he intends to give us an idea, by lively and affecting deſcription, ſo as to make us in a manner ſee every thing he deſcribes. The Painter exhibits the repreſentation of theſe objects to us upon canvas; and, by the happy union of light and ſhade, and the ſtrange illuſion of colours, deceives us almoſt into a belief of the reality of their exiſtence. Both artiſts muſt have their imaginations impreſſed with a very vivid idea of the objects they intend to repreſent, and this idea muſt fill and occupy their minds; but a greater compaſs of Fancy is required in the Poet than in the Painter; becauſe a greater variety of ideas muſt neceſſarily paſs in ſucceſ-

ſion

of his piece from an authentic or traditionary

ſion through his mind, which he muſt aſſociate, compound and disjoin, as occaſion may require. A multitude of fleeting objects glide before his imagination at once, of which he muſt catch the evaneſcent forms: he muſt at the ſame time comprehend theſe in one inſtantaneous glance of thought, and delineate them as they riſe and diſappear, in ſuch a manner as to give them a kind of ſtability in deſcription. While the fertility and extent of the Poet's fancy is diſcovered by the croud of ideas which pour in upon his mind from all quarters, and which he raiſes by a ſort of magical inchantment, he has likewiſe occaſion for the niceſt Judgment in ſelecting, combining and arranging theſe ideas in their proper claſſes. Being obliged to deſcribe objects and events, not only as they appear to a ſuperficial obſerver, but with all thoſe concomitant circumſtances which eſcape common notice, and in connection with their cauſes and conſequences, he is under a neceſſity of employing the utmoſt extent of Imagination in repreſenting the former, and the utmoſt acuteneſs of the reaſoning faculty in tracing the latter.

On the other hand, the whole attention of the Painter is ingroſſed by that ſingle idea, whatever it may be, which he intends to expreſs in his picture. It is true, a piece of hiſtory-painting admits of great variety in the attitude, air, features and paſſions of the different figures which compoſe it; and conſequently,

ary relation of ſome important event, which forms

INVENTION and DESIGN; the former of which comprehends the general diſpoſition of the work, and the whole ſymmetry of it taken together, the latter the particular poſture of the ſeveral figures, and their different characters as diſtinguiſhed from each other by their correſponding ſignatures in the countenance, will require a conſiderable compaſs of Imagination; becauſe the Painter, before he begins to work on his piece, muſt include theſe circumſtances in one general idea, and give proper attention to them in his progreſs: but while he is employed in a particular department of the work, in expreſſing the peculiar character or paſſion of any individual figure, he collects his attention, fixes it on a ſingle point, on the image which is preſent to his mind; and he delineates upon the cloth the very tranſcript of his thought. Thus he proceeds gradually, in expreſſing one idea after another, till he has finiſhed his piece; to execute which requires indeed a vivid and vigorous Imagination, but not ſo extenſive a one as is neceſſary to form an excellent Poet.

With regard to the reſpective effects of Poetry and Painting, it muſt be confeſſed, that the art of the Painter generally produces the greateſt and moſt agreeable deception; as the materials he employs contribute to the fallacy of the ſenſes, and are admirably calculated to aſſiſt the Imagination in impoſing upon itſelf. Hence the pleaſure we derive from the view of a fine picture

forms the groundwork of the picture, as it does

---

picture is immediate; while the ſubſequent ſatisfaction which we feel, in diſcovering the juſtneſs of the imitation, and its reſemblance to the original, increaſes that pleaſure.

To compenſate this advantage however, which Painting has over her ſiſter art, Poetry may boaſt another, in which the former muſt yield the preeminence. If the Painter has the happineſs to exhibit a ſtronger likeneſs in thoſe features he endeavours to expreſs, the Poet preſents us with a more complete reſemblance of the whole figure taken together; for in many caſes, words may deſcribe what colours cannot paint. We ſhall illuſtrate this obſervation by an example: Suppoſe a Painter was deſired to repreſent upon canvas the celebrated Interview between ALEXANDER and the Mother and Queen of DARIUS, after the battle of *Iſſus*. In ſuch a draught he would temper the fierceneſs of the Conqueror with the generous humanity of the Hero, who ſympathiſes with the miſeries of the unfortunate. In the countenances of the ſorrowful Queens would appear that dignity of diſtreſs which was ſuitable to their ſituation, and that profound reſpect which the preſence of their royal viſitant was calculated to inſpire. But hiſtory informs us, that after mutual compliments were over, ALEXANDER diſcovered ſo much generoſity, mildneſs, and compaſſion in his behaviour to them, as to conciliate their eſteem and con-

 fidence,

does of the poem. The ſuperſtructure how-

ever

---

fidence, as well as to excite their admiration and gratitude. Theſe unexpected offices of kindneſs could not fail to diffuſe that joy over the countenance, which is the effect of a pleaſing ſurpriſe, and which conſequently ought to have been expreſſed by the Artiſt, had it been practicable to blend the air of reſpectful humility and dejected melancholy, with that of unſuſpecting confidence and undiſſembled gratitude. That this could not be done, muſt be imputed, not to the fault of the Painter, but to the imperfection of his art; or rather, to an impoſſibility in the nature of the thing, of giving different and oppoſite expreſſions to the countenances of the ſame perſons in the ſame picture. To do this, the Painter muſt give us two diſtinct pictures; whereas the Poet can, in one and the ſame relation, give us a lively idea of all the different emotions of the human heart; or rather can make us feel thoſe emotions he ſo pathetically deſcribes. We may farther obſerve, that in order to form a proper notion of a piece of HISTORY PAINTING, it is neceſſary we ſhould not only be well acquainted with thoſe hiſtorical transactions which the ingenious Artiſt intends, by the moſt ſtriking repreſentation, to recal to our remembrance; but we muſt likewiſe keep in mind the preciſe inſtant of time when they are ſuppoſed to have happened; becauſe by not knowing, or not attending to this circumſtance, the beauty and emphaſis of the execution is intirely loſt to us.

We

ever muſt in both caſes be the work of those

We ſhall conclude this note, which we are afraid is already ſwelled to too great a length, with remarking, that every poſſible event, with every poſſible circumſtance, may be deſcribed by language, though they cannot be delineated by colours. Let us alſo illuſtrate this remark by an example: Imagine a Painter ſet to work on a deſcriptive piece, that, for inſtance, of a Storm at Sea. In order to give us a ſuitable idea of this dreadful ſcene, he paints the foming billows daſhing againſt the ſides of the veſſel, ſome of them overwhelming her, while ſhe is juſt ready to burſt aſunder with the impetuous ſhock of conflicting elements. We ſee her ſtripped of her rigging, her maſts broken, the ſhip herſelf laid almoſt on her ſide, by the violence of the tempeſt; and we perceive terror, amazement and deſpair, impreſſed on the ghaſtly countenances of the diſtracted mariners. Even thus far the repreſentation is lively; but the Poet goes farther. He introduces ſome great and uncommon incidents, which heighten the horrors of the ſcene, and which the ableſt Painter, from the unavoidable defect of his art, can never exhibit. He makes the lightening flaſh, and the thunder rore. He repreſents the tottering bark, at one time as raiſed by the billows to the clouds, at another as plunged into the unfathomable depths of the ocean; while, to complete the diſmal and terrific ſcene, he deſcribes the piercing ſhrieks and dying mones of the deſpairing ſailors. If any one ſhould queſtion the ſu-

 periority

those ingenious Artists themselves In the design and ordonnance of the one, and in the contrivance of incidents and exhibition of characters in the other, great scope is afforded for the exercise of the inventive faculty. Much is to be imagined, and much to be described. In order to obtain a clear idea of the greatness and originality of Genius requisite to finish a piece of history-painting with reputation, it will be necessary to recur to an example. Let us suppose a man of elevated Genius in this profession, employing his pencil on the celebrated subject of PAUL preaching at *Athens*, which has immortalised the fame of RAPHAEL. Instead of copying after this ad-

periority of Poetry over Painting, at least in descriptive pieces, in which indeed its superiority is chiefly manifested, let him read the description of a storm in the first book of the *Æneid*, or in a poem, intitled, *The Shipwreck*, compared with sea-pieces of this kind, drawn by the ablest Masters in the art of Painting, and he will perhaps find reason to dismiss his doubts.

mired

mired Artift, we fuppofe him to fketch out and execute the whole piece by the mere ftrength and fertility of his own imagination, taking the groundwork only from the facred Writings. The account which the infpired Writer gives, though comprehenfive, is but fhort; the Painter muft imagine the reft. He would no doubt reprefent the eloquent Apoftle as ftanding on the fummit of *Mars* hill, in an erect pofture, with his hands extended, and his countenance impreffed with a folemn earneftnefs and ardent zeal, convincing the *Athenians* of their fuperftition, adjuring them to renounce it, and to believe in thofe divine doctrines, and practife thofe excellent precepts, which, by the authority and in the name of his Mafter, he delivered to them. The air and attitude of this affecting Preacher would be awful, energetic and divine: they would be greatly venerable, yet ftrongly perfuafive. On the other hand, the audience would appear affected in the moft different ways imaginable. In the countenances of many of them, we ſhould diſcover a fixed and thoughtful attention; in thoſe of a few others, notwithſtanding the eloquence of the Sermon, that levity and curioſity, which were ſo characteriſtical of the *Athenian* people. In the countenances of ſome, we ſhould diſcern the ſcornful ſneer of contempt, or the ſupercilious frown of disdain; while a conſiderable number of them would exhibit in their ghaſtly viſages terror, confuſion and anguiſh, the evident marks of convicted and ſelf-condemning guilt. We ſhould diſtinguiſh in ſome the confirmed obſtinacy of infidelity; in others, the heſitating ſuſpenſe of doubt; in others, the yielding compliance of aſſent; in others, the ſpirited ardor of hope; in others, the elevated joy of exultation.

From the invention of ſuch a group of figures, and ſuch a diverſity of characters; from the happy expreſſion of ſo great a variety of oppoſite paſſions; we infer the vivacity, the ſtrength, the originality, and the

the extent of the Artiſt's Genius. To expreſs any one paſſion juſtly, is a certain proof that he is poſſeſſed of a lively Imagination; but to be able to expreſs ſuch a number of contrary ones, all of which have been conceived by the creative power of his own fancy, is an infallible indication of a Genius truly COMPREHENSIVE and ORIGINAL. In ſuch an attempt, the Artiſt muſt draw all his ſtores from himſelf; he muſt invent the figures which compoſe the picture; deſign their different attitudes; and expreſs the variety of paſſions diſcernible in them, with juſtneſs and force. By accompliſhing theſe purpoſes, the illuſion is rendered complete. Every figure in the piece is animated with nature, and fluſhed with life; and the whole painting, taken together, at once delights the imagination, and ſpeaks to the heart †.

We

† That excellent Critic, whom we have had ſuch frequent occaſion to quote, ſeems to think, that, in ſome

We ſhall only farther obſerve on this ſubject, that though ORIGINAL GENIUS is diſplayed in the higheſt degree and in the nobleſt ſphere in HISTORY-PAINTING, yet it may ſometimes be diſcovered, in no inconſiderable meaſure, in DESCRIPTIVE PIECES; at leaſt where the ingenious Artiſt, inſtead of copying real objects, exhibits, as in the former caſe, ſuch as are the mere creation of his own fancy. Even Landſcapes, Groteſques, and pieces of ſtill Life, when they are invented by this plaſtic power of the mind, and not imitated from ſcenes that actually exiſt, indicate an originality

---

ſome caſes, a good picture may produce a ſtronger effect upon the mind of the ſpectator, than a good oration upon the mind of the hearer. Speaking of the efficacy of geſture and action, he obſerves;

"Nec mirum ſi iſta, quæ tamen in aliquo ſunt poſita motu, tantum in animis valent; quum pictura, tacens opus & habitus ſemper ejuſdem, ſic in intimos penetret affectus, ut ipſam vim dicendi nonnunquam ſuperare videatur." QUINTIL. *Inſtit.* lib. ii. cap. 3.

of

of Genius ſuitable to the objects on which it is employed.

Thus we have ſeen what thoſe branches in the art of Painting are, in which original Genius will diſcover itſelf; and how, and in what degree, it will exert itſelf in thoſe branches. Let us next conſider how far this ſingular talent may be diſplayed in the art of Eloquence, and what its efforts will probably be in that art.

ARISTOTLE, that acute Philoſopher as well as judicious Critic, hath defined RHETORIC to be the power of diſcovering in every ſubject the topics moſt ſuitably adapted to the purpoſes of perſuaſion *. This definition appears to be juſt in general, as it includes the principal object of Eloquence, which is doubtleſs to perſuade, by

* Εϛω δε ἡ ῥητορικη δυναμις περι ἑκαϛον τȣ θεωρησαι το ενδεχομενον πιθανον. ARISTOT. lib. i. cap. 2.

convincing

convincing the judgment, and influencing the paſſions. To attain this object, a variety of qualifications, rarely united in one perſon, are requiſite. An extenſive and exuberant imagination, a penetrating judgment, an intimate acquaintance with human nature, with the various tempers and paſſions of mankind *, and their various operations, muſt concur to form the accompliſhed Orator †. Beſides theſe fundamental qualifications, an exquiſite ſenſibility of paſſion, an ardent, impetuous, and

* "Quis enim neſcit maximam vim exiſtere Orato-
" ris in hominum mentibus, vel ad iram, aut ad odium,
" aut dolorem incitandis, vel ab hiſce iiſdem permoti-
" onibus ad lenitatem, miſericordiamque revocandis?
" quæ niſi qui naturas hominum, vimque omnem hu-
" manitatis, cauſasque eas, quibus mentes aut incitan-
" tur, aut reflectuntur, penitus perſpexerit; dicendo,
" quod volet, perficere non poterit." CICERO *de Oratore*, lib. i. cap. 12.

† Thoſe who are deſirous to know the various qualifications requiſite to form a complete Orator, may conſult the fifth chapter of the firſt book of CICERO *de Oratore*.

overpowering

overpowering enthusiasm of imagination, are essentially requisite to a mastery and success in the rhetorical art, and particularly distinguish an ORIGINAL GENIUS in that profession †. By possessing the first of these qualities, the Orator is enabled to feel every sentiment which he utters, and participate every emotion which he describes. By possessing the last, in conjunction with the other, he is enabled, by a torrent of rapid eloquence, to convey to the hearts of his hearers, those strong and enthusiastic feelings, by which he is himself actuated.

---

† CICERO, considering the causes why so few eminent Orators have appeared in any age or country, accounts for the fact from the inconceivable difficulty of attaining distinguished excellence in Eloquence:

"Quis enim aliud in maxima discentium multitudine, summa magistrorum copia, præstantissimis hominum ingeniis, infinita causarum varietate, amplissimis Eloquentiæ propositis præmiis, esse causæ putet, nisi rei quandam incredibilem magnitudinem, ac difficultatem?" *De Oratore*, lib. i. cap. 5.

We

We may farther observe, that a person endued with an ORIGINAL GENIUS for Eloquence, will at one glance, by a kind of intuition, distinguish and select the most proper, as well as most powerful topics of persuasion on every subject, and will urge them with irresistible energy. These topics will, for the most part, be very extraordinary, and altogether unexpected; but they will constantly produce the intended effect. They will operate upon the mind by surprise; they will strike like lightening, and penetrate the heart at once.

We shall produce a few instances of this impassioned and persuasive Eloquence, from those illustrious ancient Orators, DEMOSTHENES and CICERO, in order to exemplify the above remarks; and shall translate the passages for the sake of the *English* Reader. The following passage is taken from that celebrated oration of DEMOSTHENES, which procured the banishment of

ÆSCHINES,

ÆSCHINES, his enemy and rival †. CTESIPHON having propoſed that a Crown of Gold ſhould be preſented to DEMOSTHENES, as a teſtimony of the reſpect of his fellow-citizens, upon account of the eminent ſervices he had done to his country; ÆSCHINES ſtrenuouſly oppoſed the motion, as contrary to the laws; and ventured to arraign his rival before the *Athenian* people, accuſing him of miſconduct in the courſe of his miniſtry, and charging him with being the author of all the calamities brought upon the *Athenians* by their war with PHILIP. DEMOSTHENES, having vindicated his character in general from the unjuſt aſperſions thrown upon it by ÆSCHINES, proceeds to juſtify the particular meaſures which he had concerted, with the approbation of other leading men in the adminiſtration, notwithſtanding the event of thoſe meaſures had been unſucceſsful.

† Vide DEMOSTH. *de Corona.*

Thus

Thus he introduces his ſpirited argumentation *.

This

* Επειδη δε πολυς τοις συμβεβηκοσιν εγκειται βουλομαι τι και παραδοξον ειπειν· και μου προς Διος και θεῶν, μηδεις την υπερβολην θαυμαση, αλλα μετ᾽ ευνοιας ὃ λεγω θεωρησατω. Ει γαρ ην ἅπασι προδηλα τα μελλοντα γενησεσθαι, και προηδεσαν παντες, και συ προελεγες Αισχινη, και διαμαρ τυρω βοων και κεκραγως ὃς ουδ᾽ εφθεγξω, ουδ᾽ οὕτως αποστατεον τη πολει τουτων ην, ειπερ η δοξης, η προγονων, η του μελλοντος αιωνος ειχε λογον. Νυν μεν γαρ αποτυχειν δοκει των πραγματων, ὃ πασι κοινον εστι ανθρωποις, οταν το θεω ταυτα δοκῆ. Τοτε δ᾽ αξιουσα προεσταναι των αλλων, ειτα αποστασα τουτου, Φιλιππω προδεδωκεναι παντας, αν ἔσχεν αιτιαν. Ει γαρ ταυτα προειτο ακοντι περι ὧν ουδενα κινδυνον ὅντινα ουν ουχ ὑπεμειναν ὁι προγονοι, τις ουχι κατεπτυσεν αν σου. Μη γαρ της πολεως γε, μηδ᾽ εμου. Τοισι δ᾽ οφθαλμοις, προς Διος, ἑωρωμεν αν τους εις την πολιν ανθρωπους αφικνουμενους, ει τα μεν πραγματα εις ὅπερ νυνι περιεστη, ἡγεμων και κυριος ᾑρεθη Φιλιππος ἅπαντων, τον δε υπερ του μη γενεσθαι ταυτα αγωνα, ἕτεροι χωρις ἡμων, ησαν πεποιημενοι. Και ταυτα μηδε πω ποτε της πολεως, εν τοις εμπροσθεν χρονοις ασφαλειαν αδοξον μαλλον, η τον ὑπερ των καλων κινδυνον ᾑρημενης.

" But ſince my adverſary lays ſo much ſtreſs upon events, I will venture to advance a paradox; and in the name of JUPITER and all the Gods, let none of you wonder at the apparent hyperbole, but let every one attend with candour to what I am going to ſay. If the things which afterwards happened had been manifeſt

This great Orator having by the above, and

---

nifeſt to all, and all had foreſeen them; if even you, ÆSCHINES, had foretold and declared them with your bawling and thundering voice, who by the way never till now uttered a word concerning them; even in that caſe *Athens* ought by no means to have altered its meaſures, if it had any regard to its own glory, to the glory of its anceſtors, or to that of ſucceeding generations. At preſent indeed it ſeems to have fallen from its priſtine grandeur; a misfortune common to all ſtates and all men, whenever the Deity is pleaſed to order it ſo. But *Athens*, having once been thought worthy of the precedence of all the other *Grecian* Republics, could not relinquiſh this glorious claim, nor plead an exemption from the dangers attending it, without incurring the blame and diſgrace of abandoning the common intereſt to the rapacious ambition of PHILIP. If it had relinquiſhed, without a ſtruggle, thoſe privileges which our anceſtors braved every danger to maintain, who, ÆSCHINES, would not have deſpiſed your timid prudence? for no ſhare of the blame could juſtly have fallen on the other members of the commonwealth, or upon me. — Great God! with what eyes ſhould we in that caſe have looked upon this great multitude, aſſembled from all parts of *Greece*, now hearing me, if things had come, by our own faults, to the condition we ſee them in at preſent; and PHILIP had been created Generaliſſimo and Sovereign of all the *Greeks*, without our having united

 our

and many other ſtriking arguments, evinced the rectitude of his own conduct, as well as of the conduct of his partners in the adminiſtration, in carrying on the war againſt PHILIP, comes next to touch upon the battle of *Chæronea*, which had been ſo fatal to the *Athenians*; and as the defeat they had there ſuſtained was ſuppoſed to be a conſequence of the meaſures that had been adopted, this defeat was, by his enemies particularly, charged upon DEMOSTHENES, as having been the principal author of the meaſures which brought on that unhappy event. The vindication of himſelf and his fellow-citizens, who had been either the adviſers or ſharers of that unfortunate, but glorious engagement, by the following aſtoniſhing and ſublime Oath, is

---

our aid, with that of the other *Grecian* States, in order to prevent ſo great an indignity? eſpecially when we conſider, that in former times it hath been always the character of the *Athenian* Republic to prefer glorious danger to diſhonourable ſafety."

one of the boldeſt flights of rhetorical Genius †.

This is one of thoſe ſtrokes of Eloquence, which produce the intended effect by an inſtantaneous and irreſiſtible impulſe, whirling away the ſouls of the

---

† Αλλ ουκ εστιν ουκ εστιν ὅπως ἡμαρτετε ανδρες αθηναιοι, τον ὑπερ της ἁπαντων ελευθεριας και σωτηριας, κινδυνον αραμενοι. Ου μα τους εν μαραθωνι προκινδυνευσαντας των προγονῶν, και τους εν πλαταιαῖς παραταξαμενους, και τους εν σαλαμῖνι ναυμαχησαντας, και τους επ αρτεμισιω, και πολλους ετερους τους εν τοις δημοσιοις μνημασι κειμενους αγαθους ανδρας. Οὓς ἅπαντας ὁμοιως η πολις της αυτης αξιωσασα τιμης εθαψεν αισχινη.

— "But it cannot be, *Athenians*, it cannot be, that you have erred in expoſing your lives for the freedom and ſafety of *Greece*. — No, you have not erred, I ſwear by your illuſtrious anceſtors, who hazarded their lives in ſupport of the ſame glorious cauſe in the fields of *Marathon*, by thoſe who made ſo brave a ſtand at *Platæa*, by thoſe who fought in the ſea-engagement at *Salamin*, by thoſe who fell at *Artemiſium*, and laſtly by thoſe many other excellent ſoldiers and citizens, the martyrs of liberty, who lie interred in public monuments, which this city, regarding them as worthy of ſuch an honour, hath raiſed to their memory and fame."

hearers at once, without leaving them time to weigh the motives of conviction or persuasion *.

The

* An Orator of common Genius would never have thought of so extraordinary a method of argumentation, as DEMOSTHENES here uses, for vindicating the conduct of the *Athenians* in hazarding the battle of *Chæronea*, and for reconciling them to the loss of it. He would probably have satisfied himself with producing precedents of the same kind, and with observing that their ancestors had fought the battles of *Marathon*, *Platæa*, *Salamin* and *Artemisium*, in defence of the liberties of *Greece*; but the *Athenian* Orator, instead of this cool reasoning, hurried away by the enthusiasm and impetuosity of his own Genius, sets before their eyes, as it were by the most sublime and striking figure, the awful shades of their fathers, who had sacrificed their lives in the cause of Liberty. By swearing by those illustrious Heroes, he raises them above the condition of humanity, and proposes them both as the objects of admiration and imitation. Nothing indeed could have been more happily calculated for comforting the *Athenians* under the defeat they had sustained at *Chæronea*, and raising their dejected spirits, than this solemn appeal to their ancestors, by which the Orator seems to put that defeat on a level with the victories

The laſt quotation we ſhall produce, from the Orations of DEMOSTHENES, ſhall be taken from his firſt *Philippic.* The Orator, having inveighed againſt the indolence of the *Athenians* in ſuffering PHILIP to

---

victories which they had obtained at *Marathon*, *Platæa*, *Salamin*, and *Artemiſium.*

Thoſe who are deſirous of ſeeing the above celebrated paſſage illuſtrated in the trueſt taſte of Criticiſm, may conſult the ſixteenth chapter of LONGINUS's Treatiſe on the *Sublime*; where that excellent Judge of the beauties of Compoſition hath obſerved, that by this ſingle figure, which he calls an Apoſtrophe, the Orator hath enrolled thoſe ancient Heroes among the Gods, and taught us that it is proper to ſwear by ſuch as die in the ſame manner:

Φαινεται δι' εν τω ομοτικω σχηματι ὅπερ ενθαδε αποστροφην εγω καλῶ τους μεν προγονους αποθεωσας, ὅτι δει τους αποθανοντας ὡς θεους ομνυναι παριστανων.

From this ſhort ſpecimen, our Readers will perceive that the Critic in his illuſtration rivals the ſublimity of the Orator. For farther ſatisfaction we muſt refer them to the above-mentioned chapter, the limits of our plan not allowing us to ſwell out the page with quotations.

extend his conqueſts without moleſtation, addreſſes them in the following cloſe, pointed and energetic interrogatories, ſo worthy of the Orator and the Patriot *.

The

* Ποτʼ ϗν ω ανδρες αθηναιοι, ϖοτε ἃ χρη ϖραξετε. Επειδαν τι γενηται? επιδαν νη δια αναγκη τις η? νυν δε τι χρη τα γιγνομενα ἡγεισθαι? εγωμεν γαρ οιμαι τοις ελευθεροις μεγιστην αναγκην την ὑπερ των ϖραγματων αισχυνην ειναι. Η βουλεσθε ειπε μοι ϖεριϊοντες αυτων ϖυνθανεσθαι κατα την αγοραν, λεγεται τι καινον? γενοιτο γαρ αν τι καινοτερον, η μακεδων ανηρ αθηναιους καταπολεμων, και τα των ἑλληνων διοικων? τεθνηκε φιλιππος? ου μα δι, αλλ ασθενει. Τι δυμιν διαφερει? και γαρ αν ὁυτος τι παθη ταχεως υμεις ετερον Φιλιππον ϖοιησετε, αν ϖερι ουτω ϖροσεχητε τοις ϖραγμασι τον νουν ουδε γαρ ὁυτος ϖαρα την εαυτου ρωμην τοσουτον επευξεται ὁσον ϖαρα την ημετεραν αμελειαν.

" When, *Athenians*, when will you act as you ought? When ſhall ſome extraordinary event rouſe you? When ſhall ſome imminent neceſſity compel you? But what ſhall we think of the preſent juncture, and of the events which have already happened? For my part, I look upon the diſgracefulneſs of our paſt conduct, to be the ſtrongeſt incentive, the moſt urgent neceſſity to free men to alter their meaſures, and act a more ſpirited part. Or tell me, Do you rather incline, according to your uſual cuſtom, to ſanter about idle, aſking each other in the forum, What news? Can there

be

The *Athenian* Orator paints the idle curioſity of his countrymen with great maſtery in the above ſhort queſtion, λεγεται τι καινον? "What news?" and the eloquent Apoſtle of the Gentiles confirms this character of the *Athenians*, by the obſervation which he made on their conduct during his abode among them. He tells us, that "they ſpent their time wholly in hearing "and relating ſome new thing." Αθηναιοι δε παντες εις ουδεν ἑτερον ευκαιρουν η λεγειν τι και ακουειν καινοτερον *. The interrogation of the Orator, γενοιτο γαρ αν τι καινοτερον η μακεδων ανηρ,

---

be any thing more *new*, than that a man of *Macedonia* has dared to make war on the *Athenians*, and governs the reſt of *Greece*? Is PHILIP dead? ſays one: No, replies another, but he is certainly ſick. What, pray, does either ſignify to you? For whatever be his caſe, whether he be ſick or dead, you will ſoon raiſe up another PHILIP, while you manage your affairs in ſo liſtleſs and indolent a manner; for he hath attained his preſent grandeur, more through your inactivity than his own bravery."

† Acts xvii. 21.

αθεναιυς καταπολεμων και το των ἑλληνων διοικων? "Can there be any thing more new, than that a man of *Macedonia* makes war upon the *Athenians*, and governs the rest of *Greece*?" is highly spirited and poignant; shews the disdain with which DEMOSTHENES himself viewed the insolence of PHILIP; and was admirably calculated to produce a sense of honest shame in the minds of his countrymen, to rouse their ancient spirit of liberty, and excite the strongest jealousy of the designs of the *Macedonian* Monarch. The art and address of the Orator is in these respects truly admirable. Every one must perceive the keen and exquisitely fine irony of the following question, Τεθνηκε φιλιππος? "Is PHILIP dead?" and of the answer, ου μα δι, αλλ ασθενει; "He is not dead, but he is sick."

These few quotations will give the Reader some faint idea of the originality and spirit, of the sublimity and energy, of the eloquence of DEMOSTHENES. We shall next produce

produce a few paſſages from the Orations of CICERO, which will alſo ſerve to illuſtrate the preceding remarks on original Rhetorical Genius.

The *Roman* Orator having, with the other ſenators, obtained certain information of the execrable conſpiracy of CATILINE, breaks forth in a torrent of abrupt, vehement, and rapid eloquence, in the following addreſs to this chief of the conſpirators, whom he pointed out to the whole aſſembled ſenate *.

So

* "Quouſque tandem abutere Catilina patientia "noſtra? Quamdiu etiam furor iſte tuus nos eludet? "Quem ad finem ſeſe effrænata jactabit audacia? "Nihilne te nocturnum præſidium palatii, nihil urbis "vigiliæ, nihil timor populi, nihil concurſus bonorum "omnium, nihil hic munitiſſimus habendi ſenatus lo-"cus, nihil horum ora vultuſque moverunt? Patere "tua conſilia non ſentis? conſtrictam jam horum om-"nium conſcientia teneri conjurationem tuam non vi-"des? Quid proxima, quid ſuperiore nocte egeris, "ubi fueris, quos convocaveris, quid conſilii ceperis

"quem

So energetic, ſo particular, and ſo pointed an accuſation, could not fail to confound even

" quem noſtrum ignorare arbitraris? O tempora! O
" mores! Senatus hæc intelligit, Conſul videt, hic
" tamen vivit! Vivit? Imo etiam in ſenatum venit,
" fit publici conſilii particeps; notat & deſignat oculis
" ad cædem unumquemque noſtrum †.

" How long, CATILINE, will you abuſe our patience? How long ſhall your deſperate fury elude our vengeance? For what end does your unbridled audacioufneſs thus triumph? Has not the nocturnal gariſon of mount *Palatine*, have not the watches of the city, has not the fear of the people, has not the united concourſe of all good men, has not this guarded ſenate-houſe, have not the venerable countenances of thoſe conſcript Fathers, have not all theſe the power to diſarm thy rage, and to ſoften thy unrelenting heart? Do you imagine your deſigns are not diſcovered? Do not you ſee that your conſpiracy is baffled by the timely knowledge of all theſe Senators? What you did the laſt, what the preceding night, where you was, whom you called together, what reſolutions you formed, is there any one here, think you, ignorant of? O times! O manners! The Senate is made acquainted with theſe things, the Conſul ſees them; yet this wretch lives. Lives! did I ſay? Nay, he hath

† Orat. prim. in *Cat.*

had

even the audacious CATILINE. CICERO, we may obſerve in the above inſtance, departs from a general rule, which, with great propriety, requires for the moſt part, that the exordium of an oration be cool and diſpaſſionate. The obſervance of this rule indeed depends upon the ſubject and the occaſion; and ſurely the occaſion of the oration to which we refer, demanded the utmoſt vehemence and energy.

The Orator tranſgreſſes the ſame rule with equal propriety in his fourth Oration againſt CATILINE, which is animated and intereſting from the beginning. Having, in the introduction to his diſcourſe, acknowledged in a very graceful manner the grateful ſenſe he had of the Senate's concern for his ſafety, he comes, by a natural tranſi-

had the daring inſolence to enter the ſenate-houſe, and to ſhare in the public deliberations, while he ſingles out every one of us with his eyes, and deſtines us to ſlaughter."

tion,

tion, to touch upon his own dangerous ſituation, the deſcription of which is wrought up with the higheſt art, as it recals at once to the remembrance of his hearers, the various labours and hazards he had undergone for the ſake of his country, in the part he had acted in the detection of CATILINE's conſpiracy *.

---

* "Ego ſum ille Conſul, Patres conſcripti, cui non "forum in quo omnis æquitas continetur: non campus, conſularibus auſpiciis conſecratus: non curia, "ſummum auxilium omnium gentium: non domus, "commune perfugium: non lectus, ad quietem datus: non denique hæc ſedes honoris, ſella curulis, unquam vacua mortis periculo atque inſidiis "fuit."

"I, conſcript Fathers, am that Conſul, to whom not the forum in which juſtice is diſtributed; not the martial field conſecrated by conſular auſpices; not the Senate, the chief aid of all nations; not the houſe, every one's common refuge; not the bed, deſigned for repoſe; not, finally, this ſeat of honour, this curule chair, have ever afforded ſecurity from the dangers and the ſnares of death."

The

The Orator then proceeds to enumerate the ſervices he had done to the commonwealth in the inveſtigation of the abovementioned conſpiracy, as well as to point out the riſk with which they were performed; a relation, that great as thoſe ſervices were, would, it muſt be confeſſed, have come better from another mouth. One is indeed ſorry to find the vanity of CICERO, which was his diſtinguiſhing foible, diſplayed in ſo glaring a manner in this, as well as in ſeveral other inſtances; but let candour draw the veil over his foibles, in conſideration of his eloquence and merit.

It would be a material omiſſion, while we are producing ſpecimens of CICERO's oratorical talents, to overlook his celebrated oration for his friend MILO, accuſed as the author of the death of CLODIUS; an oration in which TULLY hath exhibited an aſtoniſhing diſplay both of his reaſoning and pathetic talents, and in which he hath united

Imagination,

Imagination, Judgment and Art, in the higheſt degree. After having proved by an accurate and diſtinct detail of circumſtances, urged with great force of argument, that MILO could have no deſign upon the life of CLODIUS, but that, on the contrary, the latter had conſpired againſt the life of MILO, in the attempt to execute which intention he was himſelf ſlain; the Orator breaks out into a ſublime apoſtrophe, addreſſed to the altars and groves which CLODIUS had polluted by his impurities, imputing the original cauſe of his death to their juſt vengeance, and that of the Gods whoſe rites he had violated †.

It

† "Vos enim jam Albani luci atque tumuli, vos "inquam imploro atque teſtor, voſque Albanorum "obrutæ aræ, ſacrorum populi Romani ſociæ & æquales, quas ille præceps amentia, cæſis, proſtratisque "ſanctiſſimis lucis, ſubſtructionum inſanis molibus "oppreſſerat: veſtræ tum aræ, veſtræ religiones viguerunt, veſtra vis valuit, quam ille omni ſcelere "polluerat: tuque ex tuo edito monte, Latialis ſancte "Jupiter, cujus ille lacus, nemora, fineſque ſæpe omni "nefario

It is the privilege of Eloquence, as well as Poetry, to employ thoſe figures which give

---

"nefario ſtupro & ſcelere macularat, aliquando ad "eum puniendum oculos aperuiſtis: vobis illæ, vobis "veſtro in conſpectu feræ, ſed juſtæ tamen, & debitæ "pœnæ ſolutæ ſunt."

"Ye hills and groves of *Alba*, and you *Alban* altars, memorials of the *Roman* rites, and coeval with the *Roman* name, ſacred groves and altars, raſed by his deſperate madneſs, and on the ruins of which he reared thoſe impious piles; you I implore, and call to witneſs his guilt. Your rites polluted by his crimes, your worſhip profaned, your authority inſulted, have at laſt diſplayed their vengeance; and thou, divine *Latian* JOVE, whoſe lakes, woods and boundaries, he had ſo often defiled with his deteſtable impurities, didſt at laſt open thy eyes, and look down from thy high and holy hill to puniſh this profligate wretch; to you his blood was due, and in your ſight the long delayed vengeance was at laſt inflicted!"

The learned Reader will obſerve, that the Author hath taken conſiderable liberty in the tranſlation of the above paſſage. As the principal thing to be regarded in every verſion is to tranſlate the ſenſe, and, if poſſible, transfuſe the ſpirit of an Author from one language into another, which, conſidering the different idioms of languages, is impoſſible to execute, by rendering

give life, motion, and ſenſe to inanimate matter. Such figures, when judiciouſly introduced and properly ſupported, give inexpreſſible dignity, vivacity, and energy to rhetorical compoſition; as they always indicate not only Originality, but likewiſe great Sublimity and Strength of GENIUS. Every Reader muſt perceive the difference betwixt ſaying that CLODIUS was ſlain by the juſt vengeance of the Gods for his profanation of their groves and altars, and a ſolemn addreſs to thoſe hills, groves, and altars, as well as the Deities who preſided over them, by a ſtriking proſopopœia, as if they were real perſons, calling them to witneſs his guilt, and imputing his death to their reſentment upon

---

dering word for word; he found himſelf obliged, in order to do ſome kind of juſtice to the original, to admit ſome tranſpoſitions and circumlocutions, which, though they have occaſioned an alteration in the order and arrangement of the periods, have however enabled him, as he conceives, leſs imperfectly to exhibit the ſenſe.

account

account of their violated rites. In the first case we are unmoved, in the last we are transported with astonishment at the novelty, vivacity, and grandeur of the representation.

We shall subjoin two short passages, taken from the end of this Oration, as specimens of CICERO's talents in moving the passions of his hearers, a qualification the most essential of all others in an Orator. One may perceive him gradually warming towards the conclusion of his discourse, till he works himself up to the highest fervour and energy of passion. We can scarce conceive an address more animated and persuasive, or more happily adapted to rouse the affections of the Soldiers, who guarded the Assembly, than the following *.

The

* "Vos, vos appello, fortissimi viri, qui multum "pro republica sanguinem effudistis: vos in viri & in

The Orator concludes his discourse with a panegyric on the virtues of MILO, representing

" civis invicti appello periculo, centuriones, vosque " milites: vobis non modo inspectantibus, sed etiam " armatis & huic judicio præsidentibus, hæc tanta " virtus ex hac urbe expelletur? exterminabitur? pro- " jicietur? O me miserum! O infelicem! revocare " tu me in patriam, Milo, potuisti per hos: ego te in " patria per eosdem retinere non potero? Quid re- " spondebo liberis meis, qui te parentem alterum pu- " tant? Quid tibi, Q. Frater, qui nunc abes, consorti " mecum temporum illorum? me non potuisse Milo- " nis salutem tueri per eosdem, per quos nostram ille " servasset?"

" You, you bravest of men, I call, who have shed so much of your blood for the commonwealth. You centurions, and you soldiers I invoke, while the fate of an unconquered man and citizen is in suspense. Shall so much virtue be banished, exterminated, cast out from this city, while you are not only spectators of this trial, but the armed guardians of it? Unhappy and miserable that I am! Could you, MILO, recal me from banishment into my native country by means of these men? and shall not I be able to preserve you in your country by their means? What shall I say to my children, who regard you as another parent? what to thee, my absent brother QUINTUS, who didst partici- pate

ſenting at the ſame time, in a very animated manner, both the loſs and diſgrace which would redound to his country from his baniſhment †.

Theſe

pate with me in the dangers of thoſe unhappy times? that I could not inſure the ſafety of MILO by the ſame perſons by whom he ſecured ours?"

† "Hiccine vir patriæ natus, uſquam niſi in patria "morietur? aut, ſi forte, pro patria? Hujus vos ani-"mi monumenta retinebitis: corporis in Italia nullum "ſepulchrum eſſe patiemeni? hunc ſua quiſquam ſen-"tentia ex hac urbe expellet, quem omnes urbes ex-"pulſum, a vobis ad ſe vocabunt? O terram illam "beatam, quæ hunc virum exceperit! hanc ingratam, "ſi ejecerit; miſeram, ſi amiſerit! Sed finis ſit. Ne-"que enim præ lacrymis jam loqui poſſum: & hic ſe "lacrymis defendi vetat."

"Shall this man, born for his country, die any where but in his country? or, if the Gods order it ſo, for his country? Will you retain the monuments of his genius, and allow no ſepulchre to his body in *Italy?* Shall any one by his vote baniſh a man from this city, whom, once baniſhed, all other cities will invite to reſide in them? O happy land, which ſhall receive this excellent perſon; ungrateful that ſhall ba-

niſh

These quotations from the Orations of DEMOSTHENES and CICERO, though they cannot give us a proper idea of the astonishing eloquence of those celebrated Orators, which it is impossible to exhibit by a few unconnected extracts, will however serve to shew the power of original Genius in Eloquence, the chief purpose for which they were produced; and that this rare talent, wherever it is found, will always discover itself, as we have already seen, in employing the most sublime, the most splendid, and the most striking figures in composition, as well as in inventing the most surprising, and at the same time the most proper topics of persuasion on every subject, which it will display in all their force, and urge with irresistible efficacy.

---

nish him! miserable that shall lose him! But I conclude. Nor will my tears allow me to proceed; and the person in whose cause I speak, conscious as he is of his own innocence, disdains the aid and importunity of tears."

It is impoſſible to avoid obſerving on this ſubject, that there is no art in which the Moderns come ſo far ſhort of the Ancients as in that of Eloquence We muſt not however omit to take ſome notice of modern Eloquence; and here it would be inexcuſable intirely to paſs over the *French* Orators, who, though it cannot be pretended that they have equaled the illuſtrious Ancients above-mentioned, have however diſcovered a high degree of rhetorical Genius. We ſhall lay before the Reader a few extracts from the Sermons of BOURDALOUE and MASSILLON, paſſing over at preſent BOSSUET and SAURIN, whom we ſhall have occaſion to take ſome notice of in another part of this Eſſay.

BOURDALOUE, deſcribing the future puniſhment of the wicked, of which he repreſents their baniſhment from the immediate preſence of the Deity as an eſſential part, inquires what is implied in the idea of ſuch a ſeparation. The Reader will obſerve that

 his

his reaſoning upon this point is ſpirited and emphatical: “ Car qu’ eſt ce qu’ d’ etre “ ſeparé de Dieu? Ah! Chretiens, quelle “ parole! la comprenez vous? Separé de “ Dieu, c’eſt a dire, privé abſolument de “ Dieu. Separé de Dieu, c’eſt a dire, con- “ damné à n’avoir plus de Dieu, ſi ce n’eſt “ un Dieu ennemi, un Dieu vengeur. Se- “ paré de Dieu, c’eſt a dire, dechu de tout “ droit à l’eternelle poſſeſſion du premier de “ tous les etres, du Souverain etre qui eſt “ Dieu *.” After having inſiſted on the certainty of the future puniſhment of the wicked, the Preacher, aſtoniſhed at the in- difference of mankind to this great truth, exclaims; “ Eſt ce ſtupidité? eſt ce inad- “ vertence? eſt ce fureur? eſt ce enchante- “ ment? Crayons-nous ce point fondamen- “ tal du Chriſtianiſme; ne le croyons-nous “ pas? ſi nous le croyons? Ou eſt notre “ ſageſſe? ſi nous ne le croyons pas, ou eſt

* Vol. V. Serm. 2.

“ notre

" notre religion? Je dis plus: si nous ne
" le croyons pas? que croyons-nous donc?
" puisqu'il n'est rien de plus croyable, rien
" de plus formellement revelé par la parole
" divine, rien de plus solidement fondé dans
" la raison humaine, rien dont la creance
" soit plus necessaire pour le tenir les hom-
" mes dans le devoir, rien sur quoi le doute
" leur soit plus pernicieux, puisqu'il les
" porte a tous les desordres †."

MASSILLON, whom we may justly regard as the Prince of modern Orators, displays great power over the passions in many of his Sermons; particularly in that "on the Death of a Sinner," where he rises to an uncommon pitch of Eloquence. His description of this unhappy man in the last agony of nature, is equally picturesque and affecting: "Alors le pecheur mourant ne
" trouvant plus dans le souvenir du passé

† Vol. V. Serm. 2.

" que des regrets que l'accablent ; dans tout
" que ce paſsé a ſes yeux, que des images
" qui l'affligent ; dans la pensée de l avenir
" que des horreurs qui l'epouvantent : ne
" ſachant plus a qui avoir recours ; ni
" aux creatures, qui lui echappent ; ni au
" monde, qui s'evanouit ; ni aux hommes,
" qui ne ſauroient le delivrer de la mort ;
" ni au Dieu juſte, qu'il regarde comme
" un ennemi declaré, dont il ne doit plus
" attendre d'indulgence : il ſe roule dans
" ſes propres horreurs ; il ſe tourmente, il
" s'agite pour faire la mort qui le ſaiſit, ou
" du moins pour ſe fuir lui-meme : il ſort
" de ſes yeux mourans, je ne ſai quoi de
" ſombre & de farouche, qui exprime les
" fureurs de ſon ame : il pouſſe du fond
" de ſa triſteſſe des paroles entrecoupées de
" ſanglots, qu'on n'entend qu'a demi ; &
" qu'on ne ſai ſi c'eſt le deſeſpoir ou le re-
" pentir qui les a formée ; il jette ſur un
" Dieu crucifié des regards affreux, & qui
" laiſſent douter ſi c'eſt la crainte, ou l'eſpe-
" rance, la haine ou l'amour qu'ils expri-
" ment ;

" ment; il entre dans des saisissemens ou
" l'on ignore si c'est le corps qui se dissoud
" ou l'ame qui sent l'approche de son Juge:
" il sopire profondement & l'on ne sait si
" c'est le souvenir de ses crimes, qui lui ar-
" rache ses soupirs ou le desespoir de quitter
" la vie. Enfin, au milieu de ses tristes
" efforts, ses yeux se fixent, ses traites
" changent, son visage se defigure; sa
" bouche livide s'entre ouvre d'elle meme:
" tout son esprit fremit; & par ce dernier
" effort son ame infortunie s'arrache comme
" a regret de ce corps de bouc, tombe entre
" les mains de Dieu, & se trouve seule aux
" pieds du tribunal redoutable ‡." In the same Sermon, taking a view of the death of a good man, by way of contrast, we meet with the following eloquent exclamation: " Grand Dieu! que de lumiere!
" que de paix! que de transports heureux!
" que de saints mouvements d'amour! de

‡ Vol. I Serm. 2.

" joie,

"joie, de confiance, d'actions de grace, "se passent alors dans cette ame fidele! sa "foi si renouvelle; son amour & s'enflam-"me; sa ferveur s'excite; sa componction "se reveille."

It is very astonishing, that while our own country can claim the honour of having given birth to several eminent Poets, and many great Philosophers, it should not have given birth to one accomplished Orator; and that, while it can boast of having produced an equal to HOMER in the person of MILTON, it should never once have produced, either in the eloquence of the Pulpit or the Bar, a rival to DEMOSTHENES or CICERO! Indeed, when we consider the great variety of qualifications, both natural and acquired, necessary to constitute a complete Orator, we cannot expect they should often be united in one person; though that this union should never have happened in any one instance in modern times, must be confessed to be really wonderful. What

is

is ſtill more ſurpriſing, is, that in the vaſt multitude of Sermons, which this age and the laſt hath produced, many of which abound with ſolid reaſoning, as ſome are diſtinguiſhed by the elegance of their ſtile, we have ſeen very few attempts at genuine Eloquence. The Author however takes a particular pleaſure in obſerving, that in ſome Sermons lately publiſhed, there are to be found ſeveral diſtinguiſhed ſpecimens of true oratorial Genius; and he makes no doubt that he ſhall oblige moſt of his Readers, by giving a few ſhort extracts from them.

In a Sermon delivered before his Majeſty's Commiſſioner to the Church of *Scotland*, in *May* 1760, by Dr FORDYCE, and publiſhed at *Edinburgh*, the Preacher, after having ſhewn in a very eloquent manner the folly and infamy of unlawful pleaſure, proceeds to take a view of the miſery attending it; in doing which he paints the voluptuary in a very alarming ſituation, in the imme-

diate

diate prospect of his dissolution. Let the candid Reader judge whether the following passage does not exhibit a very striking picture of the state of an abandoned Libertine in that awful crisis: "O the shudderings, "the strong reluctance, the unimaginable "convulsions that seize his nature, as he "stands lingering on the tremendous preci- "pice! He wishes for annihilation, which "he often tried to believe in, but could "never seriously be convinced of. The "dreadful alternative intirely misgives him. "He meditates the devouring abyss of eter- "nity: he recoils as he eyes it." There is a particular propriety in the short sentences which conclude this passage; and they are as strongly expressive of the situation they are intended to describe, as any I ever remember to have read. After finishing the description in a few more sentences, the Author very naturally and very emphatically asks, "Is this the man that laughed the "children of wisdom and temperance to "scorn? Is he of the same opinion, think

"ye,

" ye, at the laſt?" Then follows a reflection, as pathetic in itſelf as the language is beautiful in which it is expreſſed: "Ah, how " different his ſentiments and language in " the bower of pleaſure, and on the bed of " death!" The Reader will find ſeveral other ſtrokes of true Eloquence in this Sermon, as well as in the other occaſional Diſcourſes publiſhed by the ſame Author.

There is a paſſage much to our purpoſe in a ſmall collection of Sermons, lately publiſhed by Dr OGILVIE; who, though he has dedicated his Genius principally to Poetry, in which he has acquired a high and juſt reputation, poſſeſſes at the ſame time, in an uncommon degree, the eſſential qualifications of the Orator. In one of the Sermons above referred to, we meet with the following bold and ſublime apoſtrophe: " O ye " immortal ſpirits! who are at this moment " exulting in the regions of felicity, with " what ſuperior indifference do you look " down on the little cares, the abſurd pre- " ſumption,

" ſumption, the inconſiſtent characters of " mankind! You who can trace the ſecret, " the imperceptible ſteps, by which Provi- " dence hath conducted you to your eternal " inheritance, muſt ſometimes look with " an eye of pity on your ſurviving friends, " dancing the ſame tireſome round of giddy " pleaſure, and prepoſterouſly aſcribing to " themſelves thoſe actions, to which you ſee " them gradually conducted by a ſuperior " hand!" This abrupt and ſublime addreſs is a noble effort of elevated Genius.

The *Engliſh* Preachers are, it is certain, more diſtinguiſhed by their JUSTNESS of SENTIMENT, and STRENGTH of REASONING, than by their ORATORIAL POWERS, or talents of AFFECTING the PASSIONS. More ſolicitous to CONVINCE than PERSUADE, they chooſe to employ their abilities in endeavouring to impreſs the mind with a ſenſe of the truths they deliver by the force of argumentation, inſtead of rouſing the affections by the energy of their Eloquence. But though we meet with no examples in their writings of thoſe ſtrokes of paſſion which PENETRATE and CLEAVE the heart at once, or of that rapid overpowering Eloquence, which carries every thing before it like a torrent; yet there may be found in their Sermons many inſtances of the moſt ſhining and delicate beauties of Rhetoric, ſuch as indicate great FERTILITY, though not equal FORCE of Imagination. Upon account of theſe beauties, SEED and ATTERBURY claim a particular preeminence. A DIGNITY of SENTIMENT, a SMOOTHNESS, and EASY ELEGANCE of DICTION, are remarkably conſpicuous in the Works of both; and the Sermons of the former are adorned with the richeſt variety of beautiful and well-adapted imagery, that I have ever met with in a proſe writer. He excels peculiarly in the application of the metaphor. Let the following paſſage ſtand as an example of his dexterity in varying and appropriating this pleaſing figure. Speaking of the advantages of a life uniformly good, he adds, " How

" would

" would this SETTLE the FERMENT of our " youthful passions, and SWEETEN the last " DREGS of our advanced age! how would " this make our lives yield the CALMEST sa-" tisfaction, as some flowers shed the most " FRAGRANT ODOURS just at the close of the " day! And perhaps there is no better way " to prevent a DEADNESS and FLATNESS of " spirit from succeeding, when the BRISKNESS " of our passions goes off, than to acquire " an early taste for those spiritual delights, " whose LEAF withers not, and whose ver-" dure remains in the winter of our days †." Having shewn the insufficiency of the mere light of nature to clear up our doubts, or remove our fears, arising from the apprehension of future punishment for those crimes of which we are conscious, he concludes with an observation, in which, by personifying Reason, he rises to a considerable degree of Eloquence: " Here then Reason was at " the end of its line; it stood upon the shore,

† Vol. I. page 296.

" eyed

"eyed the vaſt ocean of Eternity which lay "before it, ſaw a little, imagined a great "deal; but clouds and darkneſs ſoon ter- "minated its narrow proſpect *." To theſe we ſhall only add one other paſſage from the Sermon in which we found the preceding, as it will ſhew what additional grace the moſt noble ſentiments may derive from a ſeries of imagery equally appoſite and beautiful. "Carry thy eye upwards to that "bleſſed place, where thy nature ſhall be as "it were caſt anew, purified from all droſſy "mixtures and coarſe alloys of human "frailty, but brightened and refined as to "the ſterling luſtre and genuine excellen- "cies of the ſoul. Here is one continued "repetition of the ſame unſatisfactory ob- "jects, and there is nothing new under the "ſun; but there, far perhaps above the "ſun, new ſcenes, new beings, new won- "ders, new joys will preſent themſelves to

---

* Vol. I. page 321.

"our enlarged view. Look then upon this "world as one wide ocean, where many are "ſhipwrecked and irrecoverably loſt, more "are toſſed and fluctuating; but none can "ſecure to themſelves for any conſiderable "time a future undiſturbed calm: the ſhip "however is ſtill under ſail, and whether "the weather be fair or foul, we are every "minute making nearer approaches to, and "muſt ſhortly reach the ſhore; and may it "be the haven where we would be †!"

The Biſhop of *Rocheſter*, deſcribing the happineſs of an acquaintance with God, ſums up the whole with the following beautiful and ſoothing reflection; which is well calculated to inſpire that ſerenity of mind, which flows from the acquaintance he recommends. "O! the ſweet contentment, "the tranquillity, and profound reſt of "mind that he enjoys, who is a friend of "God, and to whom God therefore is a

† Vol. I. page 345.

"friend

"friend; who hath gotten loose from all "meaner pursuits, and is regardless of all "lower advantages that interfere with his "desire of knowing and loving God, and of "being known and beloved by him; who "lives as in his sight always, looks up to "him in every step of his conduct, imitates "him to the best of his power, believes him "without doubt, and obeys him without re-"serve *," *&c.* In his Sermon on the anniversary of the Martyrdom of King CHARLES the First, he conveys to us a lively idea of the sufferings of that unhappy Prince, by a sublime metaphor: "The passage through "this *Red-sea* was bloody, but short; a di-"vine Hand strengthened him in it, and "conducted him through it; and he soon "reached the shore of bliss and immorta-"lity †."

* ATTERBURY's Sermons, vol. II. p. 198.

† *Ibid.* vol. IV. p. 13.

To the examples above produced, I take the liberty to ſubjoin one other paſſage of a different kind; but which, by every real judge, will be acknowledged to deſerve a diſtinguiſhed regard, ſince it is animated with all the boldneſs and enthuſiaſm of the Orator and the Patriot. The paſſage I have in my eye, is ſaid to have been part of a ſpeech delivered in the *Britiſh* Senate, by a late great Commoner, upon a very popular occaſion; and that it is conceived in an high ſtile of Eloquence, I will venture to affirm. "I never "feared any man, nor paid court to any ſet "of men. I have worſhipped the Goddeſs "Liberty alone, ever ſince I drew my breath. "I hope to do ſo in a land of liberty while "that breath remains. And when the ſpirit "ſhall have forſaken this crazy tabernacle, "I pray my Guardian Angel to throw my "aſhes on that ſpot of the globe where Free-"dom reigns." What the effect of this part of the ſpeech was in the *Britiſh* Senate, I have not heard; but I am well perſuaded that it would have been applauded in the *Roman* Forum,

Forum, or by an *Athenian* Aſſembly; and though perhaps it is of too elevated a kind to ſuit the cold and correct Genius of a modern Critic, it would have afforded a ſubject of Panegyric to LONGINUS or QUINTILIAN.

It is not our preſent buſineſs to inquire into the cauſes of our deficiency in Oratory, as we intend, in a following ſection, to hazard ſome reflections on the ſubject. In the mean time we may obſerve in general, that moſt of our modern pretenders to Eloquence ſeem to have conſidered mankind in the ſame light in which VOLTAIRE regarded the celebrated Dr CLARKE, as mere reaſoning machines: they ſeem to have conſidered them as purely intellectual, void of paſſion and ſenſibility. This ſtrange miſtake may perhaps be ſuppoſed to be partly the effect of the philoſophical ſpirit of the times, which, like all other prevailing modes, is ſubject to its deliriums; certain however it is, that while man remains a compound being, conſiſting of reaſon and paſſion, his actions will always be prompted by the latter, in whatever degree his opinions may be influenced by the former. So long however as men continue ignorant of the nature, and indifferent to the ſtudy of Eloquence, there is little reaſon to hope for the diſplay of Originality of GENIUS in this noble art. Nevertheleſs if we conſider its nature, its extent, and the improvements of which it is ſuſceptible, we ſhall have abundant reaſon to conclude, that this talent may ſtill be diſplayed to the utmoſt advantage, as doubtleſs it will be in every age, when circumſtances concur to favour its exertion. There are innumerable avenues to the human heart, innumerable methods of captivating the affections, of rouſing the paſſions, and influencing the will; and powerful as was the eloquence of DEMOSTHENES and CICERO, thoſe great Orators, with all their admirable invention, have not exhauſted all the treaſures of their art. It will indeed be extremely difficult to invent means of raiſing and allaying, of ſoothing

and

and irritating, of agitating and inflaming the paſſions of mankind, different from what have been practiſed by thoſe immortal Orators above-mentioned; and perhaps it will be ſtill more difficult to improve the means which they have invented and ſo ſucceſsfully uſed. To accompliſh theſe purpoſes however is certainly not impoſſible *, and therefore ought not to be deſpaired of.

Let us in the next place obſerve the efforts of ORIGINAL GENIUS in Muſic †.

The

* "Sed cur deficiat animus? Natura enim perfectum "Oratorem eſſe non prohibet: turpiterque deſperatur "quicquid fieri poteſt." QUINTIL. *Inſtit.* lib. i. cap. 10.

† Muſic appears to have been in great eſteem among the ancients. QUINTILIAN in particular beſtows the higheſt encomiums on this divine art; and tells us, that it was cultivated by the greateſt and wiſeſt men of antiquity:

The talents of a PERFORMER, and a MASTER and COMPOSER of Music, are very different. To constitute the first, a nice musical ear, and a dexterity of performance acquired by habit, are the sole requisites. To constitute the last, not only a nice musical ear, but an exquisite sensibility of passion, together with a peculiar CONFORMA-

---

" Nam quis ignorat Musicen (ut de hac primum " loquar) tantum jam illis antiquis temporibus non " studii modo, verum etiam venerationis habuisse, ut " iidem & Musici & vates, & sapientes judicarentur? " Mittam alios: Orpheus & Linus; quorum utrum- " que Diis genitum, alterum vero quod rudes quoque " atque agrestes animos admiratione mulceret, non " feras modo, sed saxa etiam sylvasque duxisse, poste- " ritatis memoriæ traditum est. Et testes Timagenes " auctor est, omnium in literis studiorum antiquissi- " mam Musicen extitisse; & testimonio sunt clarissimi " Poetæ, apud quos inter regalia convivia laudes He- " roum ac Deorum ad citharas canebantur." *Instit.* lib. i. cap. 10.

The same Author justly observes, in another part of his excellent Work, that the pleasure which we derive from Music is founded in nature: " Natura ducimur " ad modos." *Lib.* ix. *cap.* 4.

TION

TION of Genius to this particular art, are indispensibly necessary. Though all the liberal Arts are indebted to Imagination in common, a talent for each of them respectively depends upon the peculiar MODIFICATION and ADAPTATION of this faculty to the several RESPECTIVE Arts. Thus the Poet, having by the force of Imagination formed lively images of the objects he proposes to describe, thinks only of expressing his ideas in smooth and harmonious numbers; the Painter, having the same vivid conception of every object, is wholly intent on exhibiting a representation of them in colours, as if he had no other method of conveying his ideas; and the Musician, having his head filled with crotchets and concords, airs and sonatas, employs his Imagination intirely in combining a variety of sounds, and trying their power, in order to constitute harmony. A musical Genius naturally exerts itself in exercises of this kind, and is indicated by them. In this art likewise it must be confessed, that considerable scope is afforded for the exertions

tions even of ORIGINAL GENIUS. Every masterly Composer of Music must feel, in the most intense and exquisite degree, the various emotions, which, by his compositions, he attempts to excite in the minds of others. Even before he begins to compose a piece of music, he must work himself up to that transport of passion, which he desires to express and to communicate in his piece. In effectuating this purpose, Imagination operates very powerfully, by awakening in his own mind those particular affections, that are correspondent to the airs he is meditating; and by raising each of these to that tone of sensibility, and that fervor of passion, which is most favourable to composition. This fervor and enthusiasm of passion, may be termed the inspiration of Music; and is the principal quality which gives it such an irresistible empire over the human heart. The maxim of HORACE,

Si vis me flere, dolendum est primum ipsi tibi.

Would you have me participate your pain?
First teach yourself to feel the woes you feign;

is

is a rule as neceſſary to be obſerved by a Compoſer of Muſic, in thoſe ſtrains which are intended to excite ſympathy and grief, as by a Tragic Poet, who would excite the ſame emotions.

We may farther obſerve, that as an arbitrary combination of ſounds can never produce the harmony, much leſs the expreſſion of Muſic, any more than a random aſſemblage of words can make an elegant and connected poem or oration; ſo Imagination, under the direction of a tuneful ear, muſt aſſiſt the muſical Artiſt in adopting and combining thoſe ſounds only, which may affect the paſſions in the manner he intends.

It muſt be granted indeed, that the efforts of Imagination diſcovered in Muſic, though not inconſiderable, are by no means ſo extraordinary as in any of the Arts abovementioned. The exerciſe of this quality ſeems in Muſic to be ſomewhat confined, being neceſſarily ſubjected to, and under the

direction

direction of the ear, by which it is assisted; whereas in Poetry and Eloquence, it is absolute and unbounded, as every idea of the mind may be described; and in Painting, it is very little restrained, since most of them may be delineated.

After all, when we consider how many ways there are of affecting the human heart by the power of sounds; how the affections may be melted into tenderness, or kindled into transport; how the passions may be raised and allayed, agitated and inflamed; how they may be elevated to the highest pitch of sublimity, fired with heroic ardor, or lulled in the voluptuous languor of effeminate luxury; we may be sufficiently convinced, that there remains an extensive field yet unoccupied for the display of ORIGINALITY of GENIUS, in the noble art of which we are treating. It is much to be regretted, that our modern Masters in this art have in general endeavoured to render their compositions pleasing to the ear, rather than affecting

fecting to the heart; that they have ſtudied the ſoft and delicate graces, rather than the ſublime and animated expreſſion of Muſic; and that by attempting to heighten its melody, they have in a great meaſure deprived it of the energy and eloquence of paſſion, and thereby rendered muſical concerts rather a delicious gratification, than an uſeful and exalted entertainment.

We ſhall conſider laſtly, how far ORIGINALITY of GENIUS may be diſcovered in Architecture.

It muſt be confeſſed, that no improvements have been made in this art by our modern Architects, whoſe greateſt ambition and excellence it hath been, to underſtand and to copy thoſe venerable remains of ancient Architecture, which have eſcaped the rage of Barbarians, or withſtood the ravages of time. Thoſe auguſt monuments of antiquity, which have been the wonder and admiration of ages, have been conſider-

ed,

ed, by the moſt ingenious artiſts themſelves, as complete Models of Architecture, from which nothing can be taken. and to which nothing can be added; and are in fact ſuch as few of them have ever equaled and none of them (whether through want of ability, or want of ambition) have ever excelled. Great veneration is unqueſtionably due to ancient Genius. The Ancients have indeed been our Maſters in the liberal Arts; and their productions deſerve our higheſt commendations: yet let us not ſhew them a blind and ſuperſtitious reverence. Abſolute perfection is incompatible with the works of man; and while we regard the works of the Ancients as ſo perfect, that we deſpair of excelling them, the conſequence will be, that we ſhall never be able to equal them: the ORIGINAL will always be preferable to the COPY. We have already animadverted on this too ſervile deference to antiquity *; and ſhall only here remark,

* Book I. Section II.

that

that this diſpoſition is highly unfavourable to the improvement of any of the Arts: and that a diffident timidity will always prove a greater diſcouragement, as well as obſtruction to Originality of Genius, than preſumptuous temerity. The one, in aſpiring beyond its ſphere, may indeed tumble from its towering height; but the other, cautious and fearful, will ſcarce ever riſe from the ground.

Where few attempts therefore are made to excel, original Genius cannot be much diſplayed. It is neverthеleſs certain, that great ſcope is afforded for the diſplay of it in the Art we are ſpeaking of, in which an unreſtrained exerciſe is allowed to the faculty of Imagination, becauſe the forms of elegance and gracefulneſs, of beauty and grandeur, which it is its province to invent, are innumerable. Where this faculty is reſtrained, and the ambition and exertion of Artiſts are confined to the imitation of certain Models invented by others there it cannot

not operate in any conſiderable degree; for IMITATION will ever be found a bar to ORIGINALITY. A pretty extenſive Imagination, we confeſs, may be exerted in aſſembling together the detached parts of one great deſign; and when theſe are united together in the conſtruction of an edifice of conſummate ſymmetry and beauty, we allow the building to be an illuſtrious monument of the Genius and Taſte of the Artiſt who deſigned it: but where the whole is only ingeniouſly collected, and no part invented, a claim to ORIGINALITY of Genius can by no means be admitted in his favour.

A Genius for Architecture truly ORIGINAL, will, by the native force and plaſtic power of Imagination, ſtrike out for itſelf new and ſurpriſing Models in this Art; and, by its combining faculty, will ſelect out of the infinite variety of ideal forms that float in the mind, thoſe of the Grand and Beautiful, which it will unite in one conſummate as well as uncommon deſign. We

have

have already obſerved, that every original Genius, whether in Architecture or in any other of the liberal Arts, is peculiarly diſtinguiſhed by a powerful bias to INVENTION. It was this bias which we may call the inſtinctive, inſuppreſſible Impulſe of Genius, whoſe ſpontaneous efforts deſigned thoſe ſtupendous Gothic ſtructures, that appear ſo magnificent in their ruins. The Architects, who firſt planned thoſe edifices, though unacquainted with the polite Arts, or with the *Grecian* and *Roman* Architecture, were doubtleſs great Originals in their profeſſion, ſince they planned them by the unaided ſtrength of their own Genius. Their untutored imaginations prompted them to aſpire to the Solemn, the Vaſt, and the Wonderful; and allowing an unbounded ſcope to the exerciſe of this faculty, they were enabled to give to their buildings that awful, though irregular grandeur, which elevates the mind, and produces the moſt pleaſing aſtoniſhment. Theſe Gothic edifices ſhew the inventive power of the human mind in a ſtriking light, and are ſufficient to convince us, that excellence in Architecture was not confined to the *Greeks* and *Romans*, but may be ſometimes diſplayed among a people in other reſpects barbarous.

Though it is impoſſible to point out the particular tracks which an ORIGINAL GENIUS in Architecture will purſue, in endeavouring to improve the art he profeſſes, as thoſe tracks are ſo various, and the natural powers of Artiſts are ſo different; yet we may remark, that after all the improvements which Architecture received in the age of PERICLES and of AUGUSTUS, it ſeems ſuſceptible of one important improvement, from the union of the awful Gothic grandeur with the majeſtic ſimplicity and graceful elegance of the *Grecian* and *Roman* edifices; and that by ſuch an union ORIGINALITY of GENIUS in this art might be ſignally diſplayed.

We

We ſhall conclude this ſection with obſerving, that though the ſimpleſt and earlieſt periods of ſociety are favourable to original deſcriptive Poetry, which we ſhall immediately endeavour to ſhew, and Eloquence will always be exerted in its utmoſt power under a Democratical form of government, during the reign of Liberty and public Spirit; Painting and Architecture will in general attain their higheſt degree of improvement, in the moſt advanced ſtate of ſociety, under the irradiations of Monarchical ſplendor, aided by the countenance and encouragement of the great and opulent.

SECTION V.

THAT
ORIGINAL POETIC
GENIUS
Will in general be diſplayed in its utmoſt Vigour
IN THE EARLY AND UNCULTIVATED
PERIODS OF SOCIETY,
Which are peculiarly favourable to it;
AND THAT
It will ſeldom appear in a very high Degree in
CULTIVATED LIFE.

HAVING pointed out the exertions of ORIGINAL GENIUS in the different Arts, and particularly in Poetry, we ſhall now conſider the period of ſociety moſt favourable

vourable to the diſplay of ORIGINALITY of GENIUS in the laſt mentioned art; and this period we affirm to be the earlieſt and leaſt cultivated.

To aſſert that this divine art, to an excellence in which the higheſt efforts of human Genius are requiſite, ſhould attain its utmoſt perfection in the infancy of ſociety, when mankind are only emerging from a ſtate of ignorance and barbarity, will appear a paradox to ſome, though it is an unqueſtionable truth; and a cloſer attention will convince us, that it is agreeable to reaſon, as well as confirmed by experience.

While Arts and Sciences are in their firſt rude and imperfect ſtate, there is great ſcope afforded for the exertions of Genius. Much is to be obſerved; much is to be diſcovered and invented. Imagination however in general exerts itſelf with more ſucceſs in the Arts than in the Sciences; in the former of which its ſucceſs is more rapid than in the latter. Active as this faculty is in its operations, its discoveries in science are for the most part attained by slow and gradual steps. They are the effect of long and severe investigation; and receive their highest improvement in the most civilized state of society. On the other hand the efforts of Imagination, in Poetry at least, are impetuous, and attain their utmost perfection at once, even in the rudest form of social life. This art does not require long and sedulous application, to confer Originality and excellence on its productions: its earliest unlaboured essays generally possess both in the highest degree. The reasons why they do so, will be assigned immediately. In the mean time we may observe, as a circumstance deserving our attention, that this is by no means the case with the other arts, but is peculiar to Poetry alone. Painting, Eloquence, Music and Architecture, attain their highest improvement by the repeated efforts of ingenious Artists, as well as the sciences by the reiterated researches and experiments

periments of Philoſophers; though, as we have already obſerved, Imagination operates with greater rapidity in the improvement of the former, than in that of the latter; but ſtill it operates gradually in the improvement of both. There never aroſe an eminent Painter, Orator, Muſician, Architect or Philoſopher, in any age, completely ſelf-taught, without being indebted to his predeceſſors in the art or ſcience he profeſſed. Should it be objected, that the art of Painting was revived, and brought to the utmoſt perfection to which it ever arrived in modern times, in one ſingle age, that of LEO the Tenth, we anſwer, That the *Italian* Maſters, though they had none of the ancient paintings to ſerve them as models, had however ſome admirable remains both of the *Grecian* and *Roman* ſtatuary, which, by heightening their ideas of excellence in its ſiſter art, and kindling their ambition, contributed greatly to the perfection of their works. Arts and Sciences indeed generally riſe and fall together; but, excepting Poetry

 alone,

alone, they riſe and fall by juſt, though not always by equal degrees: ſometimes advancing with quicker progreſs to the ſummit of excellence, ſometimes declining from it by ſlower ſteps; in proportion to the different degrees of Genius, and application with which they are cultivated, conſidered in connection with thoſe external cauſes, which promote or obſtruct their improvement. It is very remarkable however, that in the earlieſt and moſt uncultivated periods of ſociety, Poetry is by one great effort of nature, in one age, and by one individual, brought to the higheſt perfection to which human Genius is capable of advancing it; not only when the other Arts and Sciences are in a languiſhing ſtate, but when they do not ſo much as exiſt. Thus HOMER wrote his *Iliad* and *Odyſſey*, when there was not a ſingle picture to be ſeen in *Greece*; and OSSIAN compoſed *Fingal* and *Temora*, when none of the Arts, whether liberal or mechanical, were known in his country. This is a curious phenome-

non;

non; let us endeavour to account for it.

The firſt reaſon we ſhall aſſign of ORIGINAL POETIC GENIUS being moſt remarkably diſplayed in an early and uncultivated period of ſociety, ariſes from the antiquity of the period itſelf, and from the appearance of novelty in the objects which Genius contemplates. A Poet of real Genius, who lives in a diſtant uncultivated age, poſſeſſes great and peculiar advantages for original compoſition, by the mere antiquity of the period in which he lives. He is perhaps the firſt Poet who hath ariſen in this infant ſtate of ſociety; by which means he enjoys the undivided empire of Imagination without a rival. The mines of Fancy not having been opened before his time, are left to be digged by him; and the treaſures they contain become his own, by a right derived from the firſt diſcovery. The whole ſyſtem of nature, and the whole region of fiction, yet unexplored by others, is ſubjected to his ſurvey;

ſurvey; from which he culls thoſe rich ſpoils, which adorn his compoſitions, and render them original. It may be ſaid indeed, in anſwer to this, and it is true, That the ſtores of nature are inexhauſtible by human imagination, and that her face is ever various and ever new; but it may be replied, That ſome of her ſtores are more readily found than others, being leſs hid from the eye of Fancy, and ſome of her features more eaſily hit, becauſe more ſtrongly marked. The firſt good Poet therefore, poſſeſſing thoſe unrifled treaſures, and contemplating theſe unſullied features, could not fail to preſent us with a draught ſo ſtriking, as to deſerve the name of a complete ORIGINAL. We may farther obſerve, that the objects with which he is ſurrounded, have an appearance of novelty, which, in a more cultivated period, they in a great meaſure loſe; but which, in that we are ſpeaking of, excites an attention, curioſity and ſurpriſe, highly favourable to the exertion of Genius, and ſomewhat reſembling that

that which MILTON attributes to our firſt anceſtor:

Straight toward Heaven my wond'ring eyes I turn'd,
And gaz'd a while the ample ſky.

Paradiſe Loſt, Book viii. line 257.

About me round I ſaw
Hill, dale, and ſhady woods, and ſunny plains,
And liquid lapſe of murmuring ſtreams.

Line 261.

Such a perſon looks round him with wonder; every object is new to him, and has the power to affect him with ſurpriſe and pleaſure; and as he is not familiariſed by previous deſcription to the ſcenes he contemplates, theſe ſtrike upon his mind with their full force; and the Imagination aſtoniſhed and enraptured with the ſurvey of the Vaſt, the Wild, and the Beautiful in nature, conveyed through the medium of ſenſe, ſpontaneouſly expreſſes its vivid ideas in bold and glowing metaphors, in ſublime, animated and pictureſque deſcription. Even a Poet a Poet of ordinary Genius will in ſuch a ſtate of ſociety preſent us with ſome original ideas in his compoſitions; for nature lying open to his view in all its extent and variety, in contemplating this unbounded field, ſo ſmall a part of which hath been yet occupied by others, he can hardly fail to ſelect ſome diſtinguiſhing objects which have eſcaped the notice of the vulgar, and which deſcribed in Poetry may ſtamp upon it a degree of ORIGINALITY.

We may add, that the productions of the early ages, when they preſent to us ſcenes of nature and a ſtate of life we are little acquainted with, and which are very different from thoſe that now ſubſiſt, will to us appear original, though they may not be really ſuch if the true originals are loſt, of which the works that yet remain are only copies or imitations. Thus the Comedies of TERENCE are valued, becauſe the Originals of MENANDER, which the *Roman* Poet imitated, excepting a few fragments,

are

are loſt. Could the works of the latter be recovered, thoſe of the former would loſe much of their reputation. Thus far the ſuperiority of Poetic Genius in thoſe early ages is accidental, and therefore no way meritorious. It is the effect of a particular ſituation. It is the conſequence of antiquity.

The next reaſon we ſhall give, why original Poetic Genius appears in its utmoſt perfection in the firſt periods of ſocial life, is the ſimplicity and uniformity of manners peculiar to ſuch periods.

Manners have a much greater effect on the exertions of Poetic Genius, than is commonly imagined. The ſimple manners which prevail among moſt nations in the infancy of ſociety, are peculiarly favourable to ſuch exertions. In this primitive ſtate of nature, when mankind begin to unite in ſociety, the manners, ſentiments, and paſſions are (if we may uſe the expreſſion) perfectly ORIGINAL. They are the dictates of nature, unmixed and undisguised: they are therefore more easily comprehended and described. The Poet in describing his own feelings, describes also the feelings of others; for in such a state of society, these are similar and uniform in all. Their tastes, dispositions, and manners are thrown into the same mould, and generally formed upon one and the same model. Artless and tender loves, generous friendships, and warlike exploits, compose the history of this uncultivated period; and the Poet who relates these, feeling the inspiration of his subject, is himself animated with all the ardor of the Lover, the Friend, and the Hero. Hence as his sensations are warm and vivid, his sentiments will become passionate or sublime, as the occasion may require; his descriptions energetic; his stile bold, elevated, and metaphorical; and the whole, being the effusion of a glowing fancy and an impassioned heart, will be perfectly natural and ORIGINAL. Thus

far

far then an early and uncultivated ſtate of ſociety, in which the manners, ſentiments and paſſions, run in the uniform current above-mentioned (as they do in moſt infant ſocieties) appears favourable to the diſplay of original Poetic Genius.

A third cauſe of this quality's being remarkably exerted in an early period of ſociety, is the leiſure and tranquillity of uncultivated life, together with the innocent pleaſures which generally attend it.

Genius naturally ſhoots forth in the ſimplicity and tranquillity of uncultivated life. The undiſturbed peace, and the innocent rural pleaſures of this primeval ſtate, are, if we may ſo expreſs it, congenial to its nature. A Poet of true Genius delights to contemplate and deſcribe thoſe primitive ſcenes, which recal to our remembrance the fabulous era of the golden age. Happily exempted from that tormenting ambition, and thoſe vexatious deſires, which trouble

the

the current of modern life, he wanders with a ſerene, contented heart, through walks and groves conſecrated to the Muſes; or, indulging a ſublime, penſive, and ſweetly-ſoothing melancholy, ſtrays with a ſlow and ſolemn ſtep, through the unfrequented deſert, along the naked beach, or the bleak and barren heath. In ſuch a ſituation, every theme is a ſource of inſpiration, whether he deſcribes the beauties of nature, which he ſurveys with tranſport; or the peaceful innocence of thoſe happy times, which are ſo wonderfully ſoothing and pleaſing to the imagination. His deſcriptions therefore will be perfectly vivid and original, becauſe they are the tranſcript of his own feelings. Such a ſituation as that we have above repreſented, is particularly favourable to a paſtoral Poet, and is very ſimilar tc that enjoyed by THEOCRITUS, which no doubt had a happy influence on his compoſitions; and it is a ſituation highly propitious to the efforts of every ſpecies of Poetic Genius.

Perhaps

Perhaps we may be thought to refine too much on this point; and it may be questioned whether ſuch tranquillity and innocence as we have above ſuppoſed have ever exiſted in any ſtate of ſociety. To this we may anſwer, That though the traditionary or even hiſtorical accounts of the early ages, are not much to be depended on; yet thoſe ancient original poems which we have in our hands, give us reaſon to think that a certain innocence of manners, accompanied with that tranquillity which is its conſequence, prevailed among thoſe people whom we are not aſhamed to call barbarous, in a much higher degree than in more modern and cultivated periods.

The laſt cauſe we ſhall aſſign why original Poetic Genius appears in its utmoſt perfection in the uncultivated ages of ſociety, is, its exemption from the rules and reſtraints of Criticiſm, and its want of that knowledge which is acquired from books. When we conſider learning and critical knowledge as unfavourable to original Poetry, we hope we ſhall not be accuſed of pleading the cauſe of ignorance, ruſticity, and barbariſm; any more than when we ſpeak of the happy influence of the ſimple uncultivated periods of ſociety on the productions of the above-mentioned art, we ſhall be ſuppoſed to prefer thoſe rude and artleſs ages to a highly civilized ſtate of life. The effects of Literature and Criticiſm in the improvement of all the ſciences and all the arts, excepting Poetry alone; and the advantages of a ſtate of civilization, in augmenting and refining the pleaſures of ſocial life, are too obvious to require to be pointed out. We are at preſent only concerned to examine the effects of Learning and critical Knowledge on original Poetry, the want of which we affirm to be one of the principal cauſes of this art's being carried to its higheſt perfection in the firſt uncultivated periods of human ſociety.

Let

Let us inquire into the effects of these, upon the mind of a Poet possessed of a high degree of original Genius. By an acquaintance with that Literature which is derived from books, it will be granted, he may attain the knowledge of a great variety of events, and see human nature in a great variety of forms. By collecting the observations and experience of past ages, by superadding his own, and by reasoning justly from acknowledged principles, he may, no doubt, acquire more accurate and extensive ideas of the works of Nature and Art, and may likewise be thereby qualified to inrich the Sciences with new discoveries, as well as most of the Arts with new inventions and improvements. In his own art only he can never become an original Author by such means; nor, strictly speaking, so much as acquire the materials, by the use of which he may justly attain this character: for the ideas derived from books, that is, from the ideas of others, can by no process of poetical chymistry confer perfect Originality.

Thoſe ideas which are the intire creation of the mind, or are the reſult of the Poet's own obſervations, and immediately drawn from nature, are the only original ones in the proper ſenſe. A Poet who adopts images, who culls out incidents he has met with in the writings of other Authors, and who imitates characters which have been portrayed by other Poets, or perhaps by Hiſtorians, cannot ſurely with any propriety be conſidered as an Original, though he may at the ſame time diſcover conſiderable powers of Imagination in adapting thoſe images and incidents, as well as transforming and molding theſe characters to the general deſign of his poem. In order to become a Poet perfectly original (of whom only it muſt be remembered we are here treating) he muſt, if he ſhould attempt Epic Poetry, invent images, incidents and characters: tradition may indeed ſupply him with the groundwork of the poem, as it did HOMER, but the ſuperſtructure muſt be altogether his own. In executing ſuch a work, what aid can a

truly

truly original Poet receive from books? If he borrows aid from the performances of others, he is no longer a complete Original. To maintain this character throughout, he must rely on his own fund: his own plastic imagination must supply him with every thing.

But such intire Originality very rarely happens, especially in a modern age. Many of the most splendid images of Poetry have been already exhibited, many of the most striking characters in human life have been delineated, and many of the most beautiful objects of nature, and such as are most obvious, have been described by preceding Bards. It will be very difficult therefore for their successors to select objects which the eye of Fancy hath never explored, and none but a Genius uncommonly original can hope to accomplish it.

There are very different degrees of Originality in Poetry; and several eminent Geniuſes in this art, poſſeſſing a very conſiderable ſhare of Originality themſelves, have however been contented to imitate the great Father of Epic Poetry in one circumſtance or another; partly perhaps through a conſciouſneſs of their being unable to produce any thing of a different kind equal to his compoſitions, partly through a natural tendency to imitate the excellencies they admired in a model rendered venerable by the concurrent teſtimonies of all ages in his favour, and partly through the real difficulty of attaining complete Originality in the province of the *Epopœa* after him. Thus VIRGIL copied many of the epiſodes and images of the *Mæonian* Bard; TASSO imitated ſome of his characters, as well as adopted a part of his imagery; and even the divine MILTON condeſcended, in a very few inſtances indeed, to imitate this Prince of ancient Poets, in caſes where his own Genius, left to its native energy, and uninfluenced by an acquaintance with the Writings of HOMER, would have enabled him to equal the *Greek* Poet.

Poet. An inſtance of this kind occurs in the end of the fourth book of *Paradiſe Loſt*, where MILTON informs us that Satan, while he was preparing for a dreadful combat with his antagoniſt, fled away, upon obſerving that one of the ſcales which were ſuſpended from Heaven, kicked the beam, thereby preſaging to him an unfortunate iſſue of the encounter. By this cool expedient, which was ſuggeſted by that paſſage of HOMER, in which JUPITER is ſuppoſed to weigh the fates of HECTOR and ACHILLES in his golden balance, MILTON has prevented the conſequences of this horrid fray, ſacrificed a real excellence to a frivolous imitation, and very much diſappointed the eager expectations of the Reader. The Poet's own Genius, had he been unacquainted with the *Iliad*, would naturally have led him to deſcribe thoſe mighty combatants engaged in dreadful fight; but a propenſity to the imitation of ſo eminent an Author, repreſſed the native ardor of his own imagination. This ſingle inſtance is ſufficient to ſhew us the effect of Literature on the mind of a Poet of original Genius, whose exertions it probably will in some instances suppress, but cannot in any instance assist. On the other hand, a Poet living in the more early periods of society, having few or no preceding Bards for his models, is in very little hazard of being betrayed into imitation, which in a modern age it is so difficult to avoid; but, giving full scope to the bent of his Genius, he is enabled, if he is possessed of a high degree of this quality, to produce a Work completely original. From this train of reasoning it appears, that the Literature which is acquired from books, especially from the Works of preceding Bards, is unfavourable to Originality in Poetry; and that Poets who live in the first periods of society, who are destitute of the means of learning, and consequently are exempted from the possibility of Imitation, enjoy peculiar advantages for original composition.

We

We may add, that another effect of learning is, to ENCUMBER and OVERLOAD the mind of an original Poetic Genius. Indeed it has this effect upon the mind of every man who has not properly arranged its scattered materials, and who by thought and reflection has not "digested into sense the motley meal †." But however properly arranged those materials may be, and however thoroughly digested this intellectual food, an original Genius will sometimes find an inconveniency resulting from it; for as no man can attend to and comprehend many different things at once, his mental faculties will in some cases be necessarily oppressed and overcharged with the immensity of his own conceptions, when weighed down by the additional load of learning. The truth is, a Poet of original Genius has very little occasion for the weak aid of Literature: he is self-taught. He comes into the world as it were completely accomplished. Nature sup-

† *Night Thoughts.*

plies the materials of his compositions; his senses are the under-workmen, while Imagination, like a masterly Architect, superintends and directs the whole. Or, to speak more properly, Imagination both supplies the materials, and executes the work, since it calls into being " things that are not," and creates and peoples worlds of its own. It may be easily conceived therefore, that an original Poetic Genius, possessing such innate treasure (if we may be allowed an unphilosophical expression) has no use for that which is derived from books, since he may be encumbered, but cannot be inriched by it; for though the chief merit of ordinary Writers may consist in arranging and presenting us with the thoughts of others, that of an original Writer will always consist in presenting us with such thoughts as are his own.

We observed likewise, that an EXEMPTION from the RULES and RESTRAINTS of CRITICISM, contributed greatly to the more remarkable display of original Poetic Genius in the

the firſt ages of ſociety. Every ſpecies of original Genius delights to range at liberty, and eſpecially original Poetic Genius, which abhors the fetters of Criticiſm, claims the privilege of the freeborn ſons of Nature, and never relinquiſhes it without the utmoſt regret. This noble talent knows no law, and acknowledges none in the uncultivated ages of the world excepting its own ſpontaneous impulſe, which it obeys without control, and without any dread of the cenſure of Critics. The truth is, Criticiſm was never formed into a ſyſtem, till ARISTOTLE, that penetrating, and (to uſe an expreſſion by which VOLTAIRE characteriſes Mr LOCKE) "methodical Genius" aroſe, who deduced his Poetics, not from his own imagination, but from his accurate obſervations on the Works of HOMER, SOPHOCLES, ÆSCHYLUS, and EURIPIDES. Let us obſerve the probable and natural effects which a ſtrict adherence to the rules of Criticiſm will have on original Genius in Poetry. One obvious effect of it is, that it confines the attention to artificial rules, and

ties

ties the mind down to the obſervance of them, perhaps at the very time that the imagination is upon the ſtretch, and graſping at ſome idea aſtoniſhingly great, which however it is obliged, though with the utmoſt reluctance, to quit, being intimidated by the apprehenſion of incurring cenſure. By this means, the irregular but noble boldneſs of Fancy is checked, the divine and impetuous ardor of Genius is, we do not ſay extinguiſhed, but in a great meaſure ſuppreſſed, and many ſhining excellencies ſacrificed to juſtneſs of deſign, and regular uniformity of execution.

The candid Reader will obſerve, that the queſtion we have been examining is not whether critical Learning be upon the whole really uſeful to an Author of Genius, ſo as to render his Works more perfect and accurate, but what its particular effect will be upon the productions of a Genius truly original. We are far from intending to diſregard or cenſure thoſe rules "for writing well," which have been eſtabliſhed by ſound judgment,

and

and an exact discernment of the various species of composition; an attempt that would be equally weak and vain. On the contrary, we profess a reverence for those laws of writing, which good sense and the corresponding voice of ages have pronounced important; and we consider them as what ought never to be violated; though with respect to others of a more trivial nature, however binding they may be upon ordinary Authors, we can look upon them in no other light, than as the frivolous fetters of original Genius, to which it has submitted through fear, always improperly, and sometimes ridiculously, but which it may boldly shake off at pleasure; at least whenever it finds them suppressing its exertion, or whenever it can reach an uncommon excellence by its emancipation.

Upon the whole, from the reasons above assigned, it seems evident, that the EARLY UNCULTIVATED ages of society are most favourable to the display of original Genius in Poetry; whence it is natural to expect, that

in

in ſuch ages the greateſt Originals in this art will always ariſe. Unhappily for us, this point does not admit of proof from an induction of many particulars; for very few original Poems of thoſe nations among whom they might have been expected, have deſcended through the viciſſitudes and revolutions of ſo many ages to our times. Moſt of the monuments of Genius, as well as the works of Art, have periſhed in the general wreck of empire; and we can only conjecture the merit of ſuch as are loſt from that of the ſmall number of thoſe which remain. While the Works of HOMER and OSSIAN however are in our hands, theſe, without any other examples, will be ſufficient to eſtabliſh the truth of the firſt part of our aſſertion, That in the early periods of ſociety, original Poetic Genius will in general be exerted in its utmoſt vigour. Let us now proceed to ſhew the truth of the ſecond part of it, which was, That this quality will ſeldom appear in a very high degree in cultivated life, and let us aſſign the reaſons of it.

SHAKESPEAR is the only modern Author, (whoſe times by the way compared with the preſent are not very modern) whom, in point of Originality, we can venture to compare with thoſe eminent ancient Poets above-mentioned. In ſublimity of Genius indeed, MILTON is inferior to neither of them; but it cannot be pretended that he was ſo complete an Original as the one or the other, ſince he was indebted to the ſacred Writings for ſeveral important incidents, and for many ſublime ſentiments, to be met with in *Paradiſe Loſt*; not to mention what was formerly obſerved, that in a few paſſages he imitated the great Father of Poetry. With reſpect to SHAKESPEAR therefore, admitting him to be a modern Author, he is at any rate but a ſingle exception; though indeed his Genius was ſo ſtrangely irregular, and ſo different from that of every other Mortal, *Cui nihil ſimile aut ſecundum*, that no argument can be drawn from ſuch an example to invalidate our poſition; ſince he would probably have diſcovered the ſame great and eccentric Genius, which

which we ſo much admire at preſent, in any age or country whatever. External cauſes, though they have great influence on common minds, would have had very little on ſuch a one as SHAKESPEAR'S. Let it be confeſſed, however, in juſtice to our own age, that if it hath not produced ſuch perfect Originals as thoſe above-mentioned, which perhaps may be partly imputed to the influence of cauſes peculiar to the preſent period and ſtate of ſociety, yet it hath produced ſeveral elegant, and ſome exalted Geniuſes in Poetry; who are diſtinguiſhed alſo by a very conſiderable degree of Originality, and ſuch as is rarely to be met with in a modern age. The names of YOUNG, GRAY, OGILVIE, COLLINS, AKENSIDE, and MASON, as they do honour to the preſent age, will probably be tranſmitted with reputation to poſterity. But ſince it muſt be univerſally allowed, that ſuch intire Originality, as we have ſhewn to be competent to an uncultivated period, hath never yet appeared in modern times, excepting in the ſingle inſtance above-mentioned, it it may be worth the while to inquire into the causes why it so seldom appears, or can be expected to appear in cultivated life.

If we have successfully investigated the causes why original Poetic Genius is most remarkably displayed in the uncultivated state of society; we shall probably discover that the chief causes of its being rarely found in the same degree in more civilized ages, are the OPPOSITES of the former. Thus the first cause we assigned of this quality's being exerted in a higher degree in the EARLIER periods of social life, was deduced from the ANTIQUITY of those periods, and the SMALL PROGRESS of CULTIVATION in them. One reason therefore why it will so seldom appear in a later period, must be the disadvantage of living so long after the field of Fancy hath been preoccupied by the more ancient Bards. We have already allowed that a truly original Poet will strike out a path for himself; but it must likewise be allowed, that to do so after his illustrious predecessors, will at least be more difficult. To what hath been above advanced on this head, we ſhall here only add a ſingle obſervation, that ſhould any modern Poet with juſtice claim an equality of merit with the renowned Ancients in point of Originality, he would, conſidering the diſadvantages he muſt labour under, be intitled to a ſtill ſuperior ſhare of reputation. In the mean time we may reaſonably infer, that the difference in the period of ſociety abovementioned, will always prove unfavourable to the Originality of a modern Poet; and may be conſidered as one cauſe why this quality rarely appears in a very high degree in poliſhed life.

We conſidered the SIMPLICITY and UNIFORMITY of ancient Manners, as another cauſe why original Genius is exerted in its utmoſt vigour in the FIRST periods of ſociety. We may remark, on the other hand, that the DIVERSITY, DISSIPATION, and exceſſive REFINEMENTS of modern Manners, will naturally prove unfavourable to its exertion,

in

in later and more civilized ages. Where there is a great diverſity of Manners, it will be difficult to mark and to deſcribe the predominating colours. Where Diſſipation prevails, Genius is in danger of being drawn within its vortex ; and the falſe refinements in Luxury and Pleaſure, which are characteriſtical of later ages though they are conſiſtent enough with, and even productive of the improvement of all the mechanical, and ſome of the liberal Arts; yet they are unfriendly to the two moſt ſublime of all the liberal Arts, original Poetry and Eloquence. An exceſs of Luxury is indeed almoſt as unfavourable to the cultivation of Genius in theſe, as it is to the cultivation of Virtue. It enfeebles the mind, as it corrupts the heart, and gradually ſuppreſſes that ſtrenuous exertion of the mental faculties, by which conſummate excellence is to be attained. Poetic Genius in particular cannot flouriſh either in uninterrupted SUNSHINE, or in continual SHADE. It languiſhes under the blazing ardor of a ſummer noon, as its buds are blaſted by the damp fogs and chilling breath of a winter ſky. Poverty is ſcarce more unfavourable to the diſplay of true Poetic Genius than exceſſive Affluence is. The former cruſhes its early and aſpiring efforts at once; the latter more ſlowly, but no leſs ſurely, enervates its powers, and diſſolves them in Luxury and Pleaſure. It was a ſenſible obſervation of a *French* Monarch *, though the conjunction be ſomewhat fantaſtical, *Poetæ & equi alendi, non ſaginandi.* The ſituation moſt deſirable for a Poet is the middle ſtate of life. He ought neither to riot in the fulneſs of opulence, nor to feel the pinching wants of poverty, but to poſſeſs that eaſe and independence, which are neceſſary to unfold the bloſſoms of Genius to the utmoſt advantage.

The third cauſe which we aſſigned of original Poetic Genius being moſt remarkably diſplayed in the uncultivated ſtate of ſo-

* CHARLES the Ninth.

ciety,

ciety, was the LEISURE and TRANQUILLITY naturally reſulting from ſuch a ſtate. The cauſe therefore why it ſeldom appears in a more advanced period, will be juſt the reverſe of the former, namely, the ACTIVITY and ARDOR, the HURRY and BUSTLE obſervable in modern ages, occaſioned by their eager purſuits, and the claſhing intereſts of mankind. As the voice of Conſcience is often drowned amidſt the clamours of tumultuous paſſion, ſo the flame of Genius is frequently ſmothered by the buſy, buſtling cares of an active life. The thorny path of Ambition, and the painful, patient purſuit of Gain, are both unfavourable, though not in an equal degree, to its native ardor. The former occaſions a diſtraction, haraſsment, and anxiety of thought; the latter an intire depreſſion of the powers of Imagination. Genius is miſled by the one, perverted by the other. Indeed it ſcarce ever happens, that a high degree of this quality is allied to Avarice: it ſeldom ſtoops to the drudgery of laborious buſineſs for the ſake of wealth, of which it is naturally very little ſolicitous, and with the ardent deſire of which it is in a great meaſure incompatible. Ambition however has charms capable of ſeducing it. Honour and Power are objects at which it frequently aſpires; and they often prove obſtructions to its native exertions in its proper ſphere, by engaging the mind in purſuits, which produce embarraſſment and perplexity. True Genius, removed from the din and tumult of buſineſs and care, ſhoots up to the nobleſt height; it ſpreads forth all its luxuriance in the peaceful vale of rural tranquillity. Its fate in advanced ſociety, and amidſt the croud of mankind, is very different. There it meets with many obſtacles to check its progreſs, and to diſcourage its efforts. Expoſed to the aſſaults of malignity and envy, it falls the victim of unmerited calumny; or, intangled in thoſe vexatious purſuits which interrupt the repoſe of mankind, its ardor is waſted in the tumultuous career of ambition, and its powers abſorbed in the unfathomable gulf of ſenſual indulgence.

The

The laſt cauſe we took notice of as favourable to original Poetry in ancient times, while ſociety was yet in its rudeſt form, was the WANT of LITERATURE, and an EXEMPTION from the RULES of CRITICISM. It will follow therefore by juſt conſequence, that the acquaintance with LITERATURE and CRITICAL KNOWLEDGE, which is ſo conſiderably diffuſed in modern times, muſt be equally unfavourable to the exertion of original Poetic Genius in thoſe times.

Having conſidered the effect of theſe accompliſhments upon the mind of an original Poet at great length, in the former part of this ſection, we ſhall conclude with a remark, which will exhibit in one view the ſubſtance of what hath been more fully diſcuſſed in the preceding pages. It is, that though the progreſs of Literature, Criticiſm and Civilization, have contributed to unfold the powers and extend the empire of Reaſon; have taught men to think more juſtly, as well as to expreſs their ſentiments with more preci-

ſion;

ſion; have had the happieſt influence on the Arts and Sciences in general (ſince by communicating the diſcoveries, inventions, and obſervations of preceding ages, they have facilitated the way to future inventions and diſcoveries, and have been highly conducive to their improvement) yet the art of original Poetry, to an excellence in which the wild exuberance and plaſtic force of Genius are the only requiſites, hath ſuffered, inſtead of having gained, from the influence of the above-mentioned cauſes; and will, for the moſt part, be diſplayed in its utmoſt perfection in the early and uncultivated periods of ſocial life.

THE END.